FAMILY VIOLENCE
IN CROSS-CULTURAL
PERSPECTIVE

D1262261

FRONTIERS OF ANTHROPOLOGY
Series Editor:
H. RUSSELL BERNARD, *University of Florida*

The **Frontiers of Anthropology** series is designed to explore the leading edge of theory, method, and applications in cultural anthropology. In rapidly changing times, traditional ways in which anthropologists work have been transformed, being influenced by new paradigms, methodological approaches beyond the use of participant observation, and field settings beyond the world of primitive peoples. Books in this series come from many philosophical schools, methodological approaches, substantive concerns, and geographical settings—some familiar to anthropologists and some new to the discipline. But all share the purpose of examining and explaining the ideas and practices that make up the frontiers of contemporary cultural anthropology.

Books in This Series

FAMILY VIOLENCE IN CROSS-CULTURAL PERSPECTIVE
by **DAVID LEVINSON,** *Vice President*
Human Relations Area Files, New Haven
Frontiers of Anthropology, Volume 1
ISBN: 0-8039-3075-5 (cloth)   ISBN: 0-8039-3076-3 (paper)

WOMEN'S POWER AND SOCIAL REVOLUTION
Fertility Transition in the West Indies
by **W. PENN HANDWERKER,** *Humboldt State University*
Frontiers of Anthropology, Volume 2
ISBN: 0-8039-3115-8 (cloth)   ISBN: 0-8039-3116-6 (paper)

WAREHOUSING VIOLENCE
by **MARK S. FLEISHER,** *Washington State University*
Frontiers of Anthropology, Volume 3
ISBN: 0-8039-3122-0 (cloth)   ISBN: 0-8039-3123-9 (paper)

CAPITAL CRIME
Black Infant Mortality in America
by **MARGARET S. BOONE,** *George Washington University,*
School of Medicine and Health Sciences
Frontiers of Anthropology, Volume 4
ISBN: 0-8039-3373-8 (cloth)   ISBN: 0-8039-3374-6 (paper)

FAMILY VIOLENCE IN CROSS-CULTURAL PERSPECTIVE

DAVID LEVINSON

Frontiers of Anthropology   Volume 1

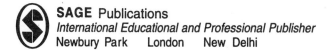

SAGE Publications
International Educational and Professional Publisher
Newbury Park   London   New Delhi

For information address:

SAGE Publications, Inc.
2455 Teller Road
Newbury Park, California 91320

SAGE Publications Ltd.
6 Bonhill Street
London EC2A 4PU
United Kingdom

SAGE Publications India Pvt. Ltd.
M-32 Market
Greater Kailash I
New Delhi 110 048 India

Printed in the United States of America

Library of Congress Cataloging-in-Publication Data

Levinson, David, 1947-
Family violence in cross cultural perspective / by David
Levinson.
      p. cm.
Bibliography: p.
Includes index.
ISBN 0-8039-3075-5. ISBN 0-8039-3076-3 (pbk.)
1. Family violence—Cross-cultural studies. I. Title.
GN495.2.L47 1989
362.8'2—dc19   88-24039
                                                CIP

93 94 15 14 13 12 11 10 9 8 7 6 5 4 3

Contents

Foreword

Cultural anthropology is changing quickly, adding new methods of data collection and analysis, and new problems and populations of interest to the repertoire of the discipline. Until recently, cultural anthropologists relied almost entirely on participant observation as *the* method of data collection, and on qualitative exposition of results. Today, in addition to participant observation, anthropologists commonly use more formalized methods for the collection of quantitative data; and, in addition to qualitative methods of data analysis, they use statistical techniques and nonmetric scaling. Until World War II, anthropologists studied non-Western peoples almost exclusively, particularly preliterate societies. Beginning a half century ago, anthropologists extended their use of participant observation to the study of small-scale agricultural societies (what came to be called "peasant" societies), and fishing peoples.

Now, many anthropologists have turned their attention to the study of occupational groups and of modern bureaucracies, as well as to the study of social problems like street crime, teen pregnancy, drug abuse, civil war, and forest depletion. The study of new problems has led to the development of new theories, and anthropologists are finding new ways to apply the discipline's theories and findings—in helping to determine the historical legitimacy of Indian tribes, for example, or in building better workplace environments, or in marketing new commercial products. The *Frontiers of Anthropology* series explores all the exciting edges of the discipline—in method, in theory, and in application—and provides an outlet for some of the most creative and controversial work in the field.

In this volume, David Levinson explores the issue of family violence in cross-cultural perspective. The topic of family violence has captured the attention of hundreds of researchers, but Levinson's study is the first systematic, worldwide comparative study of all the major forms of family violence, including wife beating, husband beating, physical punishment of children, and sibling violence. Levinson relies on statistical data to show patterns and similarities across societies, and on ethnographic data to highlight cross-cultural differences.

Levinson's study is based on an exhaustive search of the literature available on 90 preliterate and peasant societies described in the Human Relations Area Files. The sample of societies was chosen to be representative of world cultural regions, and the data were extracted and coded by a team of trained professional coders. No cross-cultural study is without methodological problems, and Levinson confronts these problems in his text. But the attempt to understand the distribution and correlates of family violence around the world is an important contribution to the topic and a demonstration of the potential for cross-cultural research using the Human Relations Area Files.

Forty years after HRAF was founded by George Peter Murdock, it has become a major intellectual resource, comprising approximately 800,000 pages of ethnographic materials on 330 societies around the world. The pages are coded, using a scheme containing 710 index categories. The ambitious dream on which the HRAF was founded was that one day, social scientists might be able to test hypotheses about the nature of human behavior and thought on a global scale. Today, that dream is becoming a reality. The validity and reliability problems involved in using coded ethnographic materials are immense, of course, and are subject to a wide-ranging debate. No doubt, the conclusions of Levinson's study will become part of that debate, but without the publication of such ambitious studies as his, and without the debate, the frontiers of anthropology would not be as volatile or as interesting as they are.

Among Levinson's interesting findings is that family violence, while common around the world, is by no means a universal problem. It is either rare or entirely absent in 15 of the 90 societies he studied. The factors that predict low or no family violence include monogamous marriage, economic equality between the sexes, equal access to divorce by men and women, the availability of alternative caretakers for children, frequent and regular intervention by neighbors and kin in domestic disputes, and norms that encourage the nonviolent settlement of disputes *outside* the home. Conversely, one form of family violence, wife beating, is correlated with male domestic and economic authority and with a propensity for adults to settle conflicts violently outside the home. This and other evidence supports both the sexual inequality theory of family violence and the controversial idea that some societies actually develop a culture of violence. Is a culture of violence a random response, or is it based on common infrastructural conditions? For the moment *that* question remains unanswered but intriguing.

—H. Russell Bernard
University of Florida

Acknowledgments

Many people have helped me conduct the research and write this book. They all have my gratitude and thanks. I wish to thank, first, Thomas Lalley at the National Institute of Mental Health for his administrative and intellectual support for the project. This research was supported by a two-year grant from NIMH. I also want to thank Professor H. Russell Bernard, the series editor, and Mitch Allen at SAGE for their interest in the book, and the care they have shown in reviewing the manuscript and shepherding it through various stages of development. Also deserving of mention are the three anonymous reviewers whose suggestions have enhanced the theoretical and methodological quality of the book.

A number of people directly contributed to the book by helping with the research on which it is based. They include M. Marlene Martin, David Sherwood, and Richard Wagner, who collected much of the data; Timothy J. O'Leary, who provided regular advice on locating obscure sources; and Professor W. Douglas Thompson, who served as the statistical consultant. They all have my thanks, not just for a job well done, but also for their often perceptive insights into the nature of family violence and family relationships in cross-cultural perspective.

I also wish to acknowledge the permission granted by the University of California Press for the use of material from *Thai Peasant Personality* by Herbert P. Phillips (1966).

-1-

INTRODUCTION

Spare the rod and spoil the child.
(U.S. saying)

When a peasant gets sated he beats you with wood;
Leave him and come home, let him bake his own bread.
(Amhara-Ethiopian saying)

Beat a woman and a horse every three days.
(Serbian saying)

Your abuse is the ring in my ear,
Your blows are my toe-rings,
If you kick me, it is my pulse and rice,
The more you beat me with your shoes,
The more we are united.
(Muria Gond-India, love poem)

These sayings from North America, the Middle East, Central Europe, and India suggest the basic reality of family violence in cross-cultural perspective—most people in the world have at some time been either the perpetrator of, the victim of, or a witness to violence between members of their family. However, while family violence is a reality of daily life for many people around the world, there are also vast differences in the types of family violence that occur, how frequently they occur, why they occur, and what means are used to try to prevent or control family violence.

In this book, I address this worldwide reality of family violence from three perspectives. First, I describe family violence by cataloging its various forms and frequencies in societies around the world. These matters are largely covered in Chapter 2. Second, I provide the results of worldwide comparative tests of leading sociocultural and psychocultural explanations for family violence in Chapters 3 through 6. Third, in Chapter 7, I discuss approaches to the control and prevention of family violence by looking at societies in which family violence is not a problem. To increase readability, discussion of methodological and technical matters is kept to a minimum in the text, although these issues are covered in detail in Appendices A and B.

The research design on which this book is based is what has been called at various times a cross-cultural survey, a holocultural study, or a worldwide comparative study. Worldwide comparative studies are defined as "a study designed to test or develop a theory through statistical analysis of data on a sample of ten or more small-scale societies from three or more geographical regions of the world" (Levinson and Malone, 1980: 3). So defined, worldwide comparative studies have a number of features that distinguish them from other designs used in family violence research, such as case studies, clinical comparisons and sample surveys. Among these features are the use of worldwide samples of societies usually numbering 50 or more cases, the use of entire small-scale traditional societies as the sampling units, and the reliance on secondary data culled from ethnographic reports. A fourth and most important feature of worldwide comparative studies is that they are truly comparative since they sample a large number and broad range of societal types.

This comparative perspective provides us with a powerful tool with a number of advantages for trying to explain a phenomenon such as family violence. First, as Korbin (1981) points out, a comparative perspective forces us to think about what family "means" and how it is defined in the social contexts in which it occurs. And, as we see in Chapter 2, wife beating does mean different things and occurs for different reasons in different societies. Second, as Straus (1985) reminds us, the comparative approach enables us to test objectively macro- or societal-level theories of family violence such as sexual inequality theory by providing a broad range of variation for the variables of interest. Third, comparative studies allow us to sample a wider range of human behavior than is possible with research focused only on a single or a few societies. For example, we are able to examine here fighting between adult brothers and sisters and fighting between co-wives in polygynous marriages, two types of family violence that are relatively rare in our own society. And, fourth, comparative studies permit us to generalize our findings beyond the bounds of a single society. Thus we are able to state with some degree of confidence that sexual inequality, or household composition, or a male sex identity conflict is or is not associated with the frequency of family violence in societies in general, rather than in only one society.

Since I have been emphasizing the advantages of the worldwide comparative approach, it is only fair also to mention its limitations. The most obvious is that by focusing on a sample composed of entire societies, we sacrifice variation within societies to identify variations between societies. Thus for example, while there might be variations from family to family in a society in the frequency with which children are physically punished, we are forced to categorize physical punishment for that society as a whole. Second, since we rely on secondary data, the data are often imprecise, with general categorizations, such as rare or frequent replacing quantitative measures such as 10% or 80%. Third, some topics, such as fighting between siblings, are poorly described in the ethnographic literature, leading to missing data for some variables of interest. And, fourth, since the focus is on small-scale traditional societies, complex societies are underrepresented. Despite these limitations, worldwide comparative studies have proved themselves over the years to be a reasonably robust design for testing sociocultural and psychosocial theories about family organization and family relationships (Levinson and Malone, 1980).

DEFINING FAMILY VIOLENCE

Following Gelles and Straus (1979), I define violence as "an act carried out with the intention or perceived intention of physically hurting another person." A family is defined as "a social group characterized by common residence, economic cooperation, and reproduction" (Murdock, 1949: 1). In our research we encounter four types of families: the matrifocal family composed of a mother and her children; the nuclear family composed of a father/husband, mother/wife, and their children; the polygynous family composed of a father/husband, his wives, and their children; and the extended family in its four forms (stem, lineal, fully extended, and joint). Our ability to examine family violence in societies with different family types is a unique and important feature of this study. Only by examining this range of family types can we test the relationship between different structural and role relationships in families and the occurrence and frequency of different forms of family violence. To give you some idea of the differences in interpersonal complexity in different family types, consider the nuclear family versus the fully extended family. In nuclear families, the only relationships possible are those between spouses, parents and children, and siblings. In fully extended families, relationships can involve the foregoing three basic ones as well as those involving cousins, grandparents, grandchildren, aunts, uncles, nieces, nephews, and in-laws in up to three generations. In Chapter 4, the possible influence of family type on wife beating and physical punishment of children is given careful attention.

The four types of family violence of primary interest to us are wife beating (frequency and severity), physical punishment of children, fighting between siblings, and husband beating. Obviously, a number of types of family violence currently of interest are not covered in any detail here. These include incest, marital rape, family homicide, and elder abuse. These are not ignored because they are unimportant or because they are not significant from a cross-cultural perspective, but because, for the first three, there is simply not enough data in the ethnographic literature to make the study of these topics productive. For elder abuse, the problem is the opposite—there is so much data that the role, status, and treatment of the elderly requires a full-scale cross-cultural comparative study of its own, such as that being conducted by Glascock and his associates (Glascock and Wagner, 1986).

To the extent possible, I have followed a behavioral approach throughout the study and have focused on the actual behaviors of the people as described in the ethnographic literature. Thus unless noted otherwise, I have not been concerned with whether the behavior is condoned or not. I have been mainly concerned with whether or not it occurs and how often it occurs in each society. The possible difference between what is allowed or prohibited and what really happens is suggested by the following description of family violence among the Cagaba of Colombia: "Aggression between spouses, especially of husband against wife, is strictly prohibited, as are physical aggressions against children. The real situation is quite the opposite of the culturally prescribed rules" (Reichel-Dolmatoff, 1951: 144). Thus if I had focused on the norms governing wife beating among the Cagaba, I would have classified them as having no wife beating, when in fact they have more wife beating than have most other societies around the world. Similarly, I am not especially interested in cultural definitions of spouse abuse, child abuse, or elder abuse, since the concept of abuse is so bound by the cultural context in which the the behavior occurs that it is not an especially useful heuristic device for ordering data for cross-cultural comparative purposes. So I am interested in behavior, not in cultural definitions of abuse or in whether the behavior is proscribed or not.

Wife beating is defined as the physical assault of a woman by her husband and includes slapping, hitting, shoving, pushing, hitting with an object, burning, cutting, shooting, and so on. It is measured on an ordinal scale:

(1) rare—does not occur or occurs in only a small minority of households in a society
(2) infrequent—occurs in a minority of households
(3) frequent—occurs in a majority but something less than all or nearly all households

(4) common—occurs in all or nearly all households.

Wife beating severity is measured on a four-point scale, based on the most severe wife beating incident reported as having occurred in the society:

(1) absent—wife beating does not occur
(2) painful—the beating is painful but causes no debilitating injury
(3) injury—the beating causes debilitating injuries such as a broken limb or burns
(4) mutilation or death—the beating causes permanent physical injury such as loss of fingers or death.

Physical punishment of children is defined as the use of physical force by caretakers in order to discipline, motivate, or punish a child or infant. Child punishment is measured on an ordinal scale, reflecting the frequency of use of physical punishment relative to the use of other child-rearing techniques:

(1) rare—physical punishment is not used or is used rarely in comparison to other techniques
(2) infrequent—physical punishment is regularly used but less frequently than other techniques
(3) frequent—physical punishment is used as frequently as other techniques
(4) common—physical punishment is used more often than other techniques.

Unlike the other family violence types, husband beating and sibling aggression, defined next, are measured on a three-point scale. Again, it is the nature of the ethnographic data that dictates how far and in what ways family violence can be studied. The data are simply not rich enough for these two variables to justify a finer distinction than rare, infrequent, or frequent.

Husband beating is defined like wife beating and is measured on a three-point scale:

(1) rare—husband beating does not occur or occurs in only a small minority of households
(2) infrequent—occurs in a minority of households
(3) frequent—occurs in a majority of households.

Sibling aggression is defined as physical violence between nonadult siblings and is measured on a three-point scale:

(1) rare—sibling aggression does not occur or occurs in only a small minority of households
(2) infrequent—sibling aggression occurs in a minority of households
(3) frequent—sibling aggression occurs in a majority of households.

Definitions of the other variables used in the study are provided in the appropriate chapters and in Appendix B.

THEORETICAL PERSPECTIVES

As the basic purpose of the research discussed in this volume was to test various explanations for family violence, it is important to use some space here to summarize both the major theories of family violence of current interest and some of the major theoretical perspectives on human society and behavior that provide the basis for much of the current thinking about the causes of family violence (for other summaries see Gelles, 1985, and Bersani and Chen, 1988). While I attempt to at least mention all major theoretical perspectives used in attempting to explain family violence, you should keep in mind that not all of these theories were tested in the research reported here. Some, such as those reflecting a sociobiological perspective, were not addressed at all. Others, which combine sociocultural and psychological factors, such as those based on the social learning theory perspective, were partially tested. And a third group, such as resource theory, which place the primary emphasis on sociocultural factors that can be opera-tionalized at the societal level, was tested. As with the selection of the types of violence to study and the measurement of those types, decisions about what theories and hypotheses to test were made on the basis of the quantity and quality of the ethnographic data available. Thus if a particular theory or perspective is untested here, it is not because I consider it trivial, but because the data are not available to test it adequately. The results of the research as they bear on these theories are discussed where relevant in Chapters 3-6.

Nine theoretical perspectives are especially important, as each in some way has either served or currently serves as the basis for recent thinking about or research on the causes of family violence in general or the causes of specific types of family violence:

(1) resource theory
(2) exchange theory
(3) culture of violence theory
(4) patriarchal theory
(5) social learning theory
(6) ecological theory
(7) evolutionary theory
(8) sociobiological theory
(9) general systems theory

Resource Theory

Resource theory rests on the notion that decision-making power in family relationships depends to a large extent on the value of the resources each person brings to the relationship (Blood and Wolfe, 1960). Resources can be either material in nature (income, contribution to subsistence, access to trade networks, inheritance, dowry, and so on) or organizational (kin ties, political alliances, and so on; Warner et al., 1986). There is considerable evidence, both from studies in the United States and comparative studies, as discussed in Chapter 5, that husbands often have more family decision-making power than their wives have and that marital power rests on the more valuable economic and organizational resources controlled by men.

Applying resource theory to family relations, Goode (1971) suggested that the more external (outside the family) resources one controls, the less likely one will need to use regular violence or force to maintain control, a notion that has drawn some empirical support (Allen and Straus, 1980), but is also contradicted (Stark and McEvoy, 1970) regarding the frequency of wife beating.

Resource theory has been revised following O'Brien's (1971) and Gelles's (1974) research in the United States and Rodman's (1972) cross-cultural research into what has come to be called status inconsistency theory. This perspective suggests that violence is more likely to occur when an individual's power or status is inconsistent (high in one social setting, low in another), or when norms governing status in the family are ambiguous or changing. These inconsistencies over space or time lead to stress and frustration that may, in turn, lead to wife beating or child abuse. Status inconsistency is especially useful as a framework for explaining family violence, and especially wife beating, in societies in which men's traditional power in the family has eroded while women's power has increased.

Exchange Theory

Gelles (1983: 157) summarizes exchange theory: "People hit and abuse other family members because they can." Exchange theory brings cost-benefit analysis to our attempt to understand family violence. The basic assumption is that family members will use violence to achieve their means so long as the costs are less than the rewards gained by doing so. In American and other societies the costs are often low because adequate social controls are not available to inhibit or prevent violence between family members—laws prohibiting wife beating, if they exist, are not enforced; shelters for abused women are underfunded; neighbors and relatives refuse to intervene in marital disputes; and so forth. And, to take the theory a further step backward to the ultimate cause, Gelles suggests that we can pinpoint certain social arrangements and norms that encourage the weak control of family violence. These include norms that emphasize male aggressiveness, nuclear family living arrangements that isolate the family, and sexual inequality.

Culture of Violence Theory

The various forms this perspective has taken since first hypothesized by Wolfgang and Ferracuti (1967) are outlined in the introduction to Chapter 3. As applied to large, pluralistic societies like the United States, the theory suggests that some subcultural groups develop norms and values that emphasize the use of physical violence to a greater extent than is deemed appropriate by the dominant culture. As regards family violence, the implication is that wife beating or the physical punishment of children might be more common and considered more appropriate or even more desirable by certain groups than by others.

The theory has been extended as an explanation for differences in the frequency or severity of violence between different societies. There is some evidence that societies around the world can be distinguished from one another on the basis of the number of different types of violence that occur (Levinson and Malone, 1980). Thus there may be violent societies and peaceful ones, and the theory predicts that family violence will occur more often in the violent ones. Of course, just saying that some societies or groups are more violent than others explains nothing. It does beg the question, however, of why this occurs.

Patriarchal Theory

This is really less of a social science theory than a political agenda, associated with the feminist perspective on family violence (Martin, 1973; Dobash and Dobash, 1979). The argument, quite simply, is that most societies over the course of their history and today are male dominated, with women classified and treated as possessions by men. Thus we expect, given this history and the continued existence of norms and laws that support this value system, that husbands will control their wives and will use violence to maintain that control when necessary.

While patriarchal theory resembles resource and exchange theory, it is important to keep in mind that patriarchial theory emphasizes forces operating at the societal level, while the other two place more emphasis on forces operating in the family. Criticism of this perspective has not focused so much on its validity, but on its verifiability—that is, the theory is stated in such general form, that it is not easy to measure the key variables with empirical data. I attempt to solve this problem and to test the theory in Chapter 5 by conceptualizing male dominance as a multidimensional phenomenon.

Social Learning Theory

Unlike the foregoing perspectives, which have their roots in sociology, social learning theory is a product of social psychology. Over the past decade, the social learning approach has replaced, to a large extent, the "inner drive" and "frustration release" approaches to aggression that had guided so much of the previous research on human aggression (Segall, 1983). Social learning theory proponents reject the notion that aggression is an inner drive, and argue instead that aggression is both learned and takes place in a social context.

As applied to family violence, O'Leary (1988) suggests that a combination of contextual and situational factors cause family violence. Contextual factors, including individual characteristics, couple characteristics, and societal characteristics, create an environment in which family violence may or may not take place. The situational factors precipitate family violence when they occur in the presence of contextual factors that also encourage family violence. O'Leary suggests that contextual factors that are especially important for spousal violence are: violence in the family of orientation, stress, and an aggressive personality style. The key situational factors are marital strife and alcohol use. When these five factors come together, violence between spouses is likely.

The approach within the social learning perspective that has drawn the most attention is the intergenerational transmission of family violence theory. There is now considerable evidence that individuals who observed or perhaps experienced family violence in their childhood homes are more likely to be involved in violent marital relations later in life (Kalmuss, 1984; Pagelow, 1981; Straus et al., 1980; Ulbrich and Huber, 1981). However, it is important to note that some research suggests that the effects of observing family violence in childhood may be somewhat different for men and for women, with a more direct effect for men (Arias, 1984). In accord with the social learning perspective, this intergenerational pattern can be explained in terms of individuals modeling their behavior on that of significant others.

Ecological Theory

As Bersani and Chen (1988: 76) point out, the ecological perspective, like social learning theory, links family violence to the broader social order:

> A person's environment can be understood as a series of settings, each nested within the next broader level, from the microenvironment of the family to the macroenvironment of the society.

Garbarino (1977) suggests that two social factors are especially significant precursors of child abuse—isolation of the family from a social support network and a belief or value system that legitimates violence against children. He also suggests that parental inexperience and inappropriate parental expectations about children's behavior play a major role in child abuse.

Belsky (1980) argues that a full-blown ecological framework is necessary to provide a full understanding of the causes of child abuse and neglect. In his model, analysis must proceed at four levels:

(1) ontogenic—the family history of the parents;
(2) microsystem—the family setting in which violence occurs;
(3) ecosystem—the informal and formal social networks in which the family is involved;
(4) macrosystem—the culture.

Neither of these approaches using a general ecological framework has been subjected to empirical testing, although a number of predictions derived from this perspective are tested in Chapters 3 and 4.

Evolutionary Theory

I now move from theories that come from a sociological or psychological tradition to one that is associated with anthropological thought and research. We now know with some degree of confidence that as human societies change over time, all things being equal, change will follow an evolutionary pattern from the simple to the complex (Lenski and Lenski, 1970; Naroll, 1970). We also know that social relations, social organization, the family structure, and family relations change in a number of predictable ways as well. Settlements become larger and more densely populated, social and economic inequality becomes more pronounced, families are likely to become smaller and nuclear in form, individuality and anonymity have increased value, and social relations become both more structured and ambiguous at the same time (Berreman, 1978; Levinson and Malone, 1980).

As regards family violence, a number of cross-cultural researchers (Barry et al., 1967; Rohner, 1975; Pryor, 1977) have consistently related differences in structural and economic complexity to differences in child-rearing practices. Caretakers in more complex societies often use physical punishment as a means of rearing children to be obedient, compliant, and responsible. Caretakers in less complex societies, on the other hand, emphasize independence and self-reliance and are less likely to rely on physical punishment. This pattern has been explained in evolutionary terms with emphasis on the fact that compliance and obedience are more desirable personality traits in societies in which people live in a hierarchically organized social structure, in which there is a continuous need to share accumulated wealth among the population, and in which much activity takes place in formal or relatively formal social encounters outside the home.

Sociobiological Theory

While there are no reports yet of research designed to systematically test sociobiological theories of violence in human families (there has been considerable research among nonhuman primates), there are theories of infanticide and child abuse cast in a sociobiological framework (Gray, 1985).

As regards child abuse, the sociobiological perspective rests on the notion of parental certainty—parents are more likely to invest resources (time, money, warmth, and so on) in their children or in biological relatives than in children of nonrelatives. The notion of parental certainty rests on the theory of inclusive fitness. Inclusive fitness theory, in very abbreviated form, suggests that individuals will act in ways that increase the chances that their genes will be passed on to subsequent generations. Investing resources in children is, of course, one way of doing that. Researchers who have applied this perspective to data about child abuse in modern nations argue that child abuse often occurs in ways consistent with parental certainty theory (Lennington, 1981; Daly and Wilson, 1981; Lightcap, 1982). Handicapped children and step-children (both have lower reproductive value) are more likely to be abused and so too are children in lower income families with fewer resources to spread around.

As regards infanticide, Alexander (1974) suggests that it may be adaptive when (1) environmental unpredictability creates a possibility that not all siblings will survive; (2) a child is handicapped; (3) scarce resources force parents to space children; or (4) parents want to adjust the sex ratio of their children. Gray (1985) reviews a number of studies using a variety of sex-ratio perspectives to explain infanticide, although he points out that none of the research is far enough along to provide any firm conclusions.

General Systems Theory

Straus (1980) suggests that our understanding of and ability to control family violence might be enhanced if we view family violence as the product of a positive feedback social system operating at the individual, family, and societal levels. Because the model incorporates in one place many, if not nearly all, of the factors researchers have linked or attempted to link to family violence, it is shown in Figure 1.1.

As can be seen, the model includes many of the factors covered by other theoretical approaches including control of resources, inter-generational transmission, a culture of violence, and isolation of the nuclear family. And, most important, the model suggests an interaction between various sets of factors as well as positive feedback of family violence into the system ultimately leading to more, or maintaining the same level of, family violence. Given the size and complexity of the model it is not surprising that it has yet to be tested in its full form. Such a test would require research with individuals, with families and across societies, a task beyond the resources of researchers today.

PREVIOUS COMPARATIVE RESEARCH

There have been two approaches to comparative cross-cultural research on family violence. In one approach, exemplified by many of the works in the collections edited by Korbin (1981), Gelles and Cornell (1983), and Eekelaar and Katz (1977) the emphasis has been on describing cross-cultural variations in family violence. These studies have provided us with valuable insights into the meanings of family violence, the varieties of family violence found around the world, and

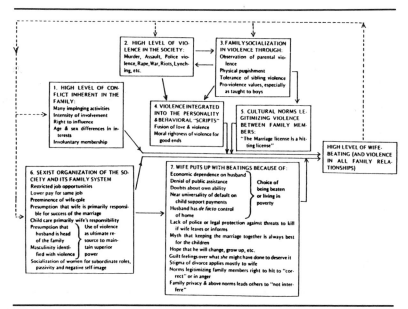

Figure 1.1. Straus Model: Flowchart Illustrating Some of the Factors Accounting for High Incidence of Wife Beating (Solid Lines) and Positive Feedback Loops Maintaining the System (Dashed Lines).

the factors that might cause or help us control family violence in specific sociocultural contexts.

Because my approach here, with the exception of the material in Chapter 2, is to look for patterns across cultures, it is worth briefly reviewing some of the key conclusions of these descriptive cross-cultural surveys. Five conclusions seem most important:

(1) In societies in which children are valued, they are usually well-treated. Children are valued for a variety of reasons, including economic ones, tradition, or because of their future role in the family.

(2) Cultural practices and beliefs determine, in part, what categories of children may be particularly vulnerable to harsh treatment. Among the categories of special significance are adopted children, stepchildren, illegitimate children, unwanted children, female children, and children of unusual births (for example, twins).

(3) There is considerable cultural variation in the definitions of infant, child, and adult and in beliefs about what constitutes appropriate behavior at different ages or different points in development.

(4) The extent to which cultural practices and beliefs provide for multiple caretakers for children is a key determinant of how children will be treated.

(5) When viewed in worldwide perspective, there is considerable variation in the types and the frequency of family violence.

The focus of this volume is largely the patterning of family violence around the world. By patterning I mean both the patterning found among different forms of family violence and the patterning across cultures between family violence and various cultural and psychosocial factors. While the research reported here is the first broad worldwide comparative study of family violence, I am by no means the first comparativist to study family violence. I have found 10 other comparative studies that provide information about wife beating for a worldwide sample of societies (Broude and Greene, 1983; Campbell, 1985; Justinger, 1978; Lester, 1980; Masamura, 1979; Naroll, 1969; Schlegel, 1972; Whiting and Whiting, 1976; Whyte, 1978; and Zelman, 1974) and there may be more. However, in seven of these studies, wife beating is dealt with only in passing in the context of the major focus of the study, such as religion or women's status. Only Campbell (1985), Lester (1980) and Masamura (1979) report tests of theories of wife beating. The findings of these studies are discussed where appropriate in the book.

There has been much comparative research on child rearing and socialization, including a considerable interest in why physical punishment is used or not used in child rearing. However, much of this literature is concerned with the effect of certain child-rearing practices on adult behavior, a subject beyond the scope of our research here. Those studies that are relevant (Barry and Paxson, 1971; Levinson, 1979; Minturn and Lambert, 1964; Petersen et al., 1982; Rohner, 1975, 1986) are, again, discussed where appropriate.

METHODOLOGY

Details on the methods used here are provided in Appendices A and B. The purpose of the following discussion is to provide a general outline of how the study on which this book is based was conducted.

The sample used here is composed of 90 small-scale and peasant societies selected from the HRAF Probability Sample Files (PSF) sample (Lagace, 1979). The PSF sample is a stratified probability sample of 120 societies presumably representative of the 60 major geographical/cultural regions of the world. The sampling universe for the PSF sample consists of all known, well-described societies of the world, about 400 societies in all. Only 90 societies are used here since systematically organized data are not yet available for all 120 societies. Two types of societies are included in the study sample. First, small-scale (primitive, kin-based, nonliterate) societies that are defined as cultural units with no indigenous written language. Second, peasant (folk, traditional) societies that are defined as cultural units whose members share a common heritage, who produce at least 50% of their own food, and who are under the control of a nation state.

The data were collected from ethnographic reports included in the Human Relations Area Files (HRAF) cultural data archive. The archive is a cross-indexed, cross-referenced collection of mostly primary ethnographic reports describing the ways of life of people in some 330 different cultural and ethnic groups from all regions of the world. The information in the archive is organized in two ways. First, by cultural unit, with all the information about each cultural unit placed together in a "file." Second, by topic within each cultural file, using the 710 index categories in the *Outline of Cultural Materials* (Murdock et al., 1982). Of course both the quantity and quality of data available on family violence and other topics of interest here vary from one society to another. However, there is enough information to allow us to measure wife beating and the physical punishment of children for the entire sample.

The data were collected from the archive by a team of trained coders. No attempt was made to keep the coders naive as to the theories being tested, but different teams were used to collect the data on family violence and the data on the independent variables. The first step in data collection was to extract the relevant information from the ethnographic reports. This was done by systematically searching through the HRAF archive for material of interest. This operation was guided by the operational definitions of the variables listed in Appendix B. The second step was to quantify the data by applying the numerical codes for each variable. Intercoder reliability was established through formal reliability tests, as reported in Appendix A.

The data were analyzed with the Statistical Analysis System (SAS; SAS Institute, 1982) and the System for Statistics (SYSTAT; Wilkinson, 1986). Unless otherwise noted, all reported coefficients are Spearman's rho coefficients. Although the sample is not a probability sample, I follow the comparative anthropological tradition and report significance levels of .05 or less as indicated by an asterisk (*) following the coefficient.

With this basic information behind us, we can now move on to family violence in cross-cultural perspective, beginning with a description of the types of family violence found around the world.

-2-

VARIETIES OF FAMILY VIOLENCE

How one reacts to this chapter depends on whether one is a pessimist or an optimist. For the pessimist, the variety of ways family members harm one another detailed here can only reinforce the belief that violence is a "natural" part of family life. But for the optimist, the absence of family violence in some societies, the relatively infrequent use of physical punishment with children, and the variety of interventions used to control violent events provide proof that family violence is neither "natural" nor uncontrollable.

The purpose of this chapter is to describe family violence as it occurs in our sample of 90 societies. Three general issues are covered: First, a review of family violence in life-span perspective, from the viewpoint of the victims or potential victims, including violence directed at infants, children, adolescents, adults and the elderly. Second, a more detailed analysis of wife beating, the most common form of family violence around the world. This analysis focuses on the frequency and severity of wife beating and addresses the possibility that wife beating is a multidimensional phenomenon. And third, a report of the results of our statistical analysis of the relationships between and among wife beating, husband beating, sibling beating, and physical punishment of children that bears indirectly on the question of the intergenerational transfer of family violence.

FAMILY VIOLENCE IN LIFE-SPAN PERSPECTIVE

Table 2.1 lists the various ways family members will harm or allow others to harm members of their family. The family violence types in the table are listed in life-span sequence, beginning with infancy and running through old age. To the extent possible, the ordering is based on the life stage of the victim. An important point about the family violence types listed here is that most do not occur with any regularity around the world. For example, binding of an infant's feet is confined primarily to prerevolutionary China, child prostitution is limited to a very small percentage of poor families in Third World cities, and co-wife fighting occurs only in societies with polygynous marriage. Similarly, some types of family violence that occur in a large number of societies, occur only rarely in any particular society. For example, infanticide is reported as occurring in 78.5% of our 90 societies, but it occurs rarely in all of these societies. Despite these qualifications, the sheer number and variety of family violence types listed in Table 2.1 indicates that family violence is something that is witnessed or experienced by most human beings at some point in their lives.

Infancy

As the relatively short list in Table 2.1 suggests, infants are an infrequent target for other family members. Sale of infants for sacrifice and the binding of body parts are limited practices that, while causing pain to the infant, are usually considered acceptable, if not expected, behavior of the parents by other members of the society.

Since infanticide will not be dealt with in any detail elsewhere in the book, some space will be given here to a more detailed description of it. The figure of 78.5% supports similar figures reported elsewhere (Divale and Harris, 1976; Whyte, 1978; Glascock and Wagner, 1986), although Minturn and Stashak (1982) suggest that the prevalence is actually much lower, at about 53% for small-scale societies around the world. The discussion that follows is based primarily on data supplied by Anthony Glascock (Glascock and Wagner, 1986) and Minturn and Stashak (1982).

Infanticide is clearly a form of family violence and is usually carried out by the mother (60% of societies) or another relative (17% of societies). In addition, it is almost always the family who decides that infanticide must be performed. This does not imply that infanticide is something that is taken lightly or performed easily. Rather, it is often performed with great pain by the mother who has no other choice. There is often no other alternative, because infanticide is a mechanism through which societies dispose of infants whose birth or condition makes them a liability to the family or to the entire group. This point becomes obvious when we consider the major reasons for infanticide. Four reasons stand out: First, when the infant is considered illegitimate, because of unknown or irregular paternity, such as through rape or adultery, about 50% of societies allow or require infanticide under these circumstances. Second, when the infant is deformed, with about 50% of societies permitting infanticide for this reason. Third, when the birth is unusual,

TABLE 2.1
Family Violence in Life-Span Perspective

Infants
  infanticide
  sale of infants for sacrifice
  binding body parts for shaping (head, feet, and so on)
  force feeding
  harsh disciplinary techniques such as cold baths

Childhood
  organized fighting promoted by adults
  ritual defloration
  physical punishment (beating, kicking, slapping, burning, twisting ears, and so on)
  child marriage
  child slavery
  child prostitution
  drugging with hallucinogens
  parent-child homicide/suicide
  child labor
  sibling fighting
  nutritional deprivation
  corporal punishment in schools
  mutilation for begging

Adolescence (puberty)
  painful initiation rites (circumcision, superincision, clitoridectomy, scarification, cold
    baths, piercing, sleep deprivation, whipping, bloodletting, forced vomiting)
  forced homosexual relations
  physical punishment
  gang rape of girls

Adulthood
  killing young brides
  forced suicides by young brides
  wife beating
  husband beating
  husband-wife brawling
  matricide
  patricide
  forced suicide of wives
  wife raiding
  marital rape
  parent beating
  co-wife fighting
  sister beating

Old Age
  forsaking the aged
  abandonment of the aged
  beating the aged
  killing the aged
  forcing the aged to commit suicide

often evidenced by the birth of twins. In about 40% of societies one twin might be sacrificed in this situation. Fourth, because the infant, despite being normal and the product of normal conception and birth, is unwanted. More often than not it is unwanted because it is the wrong sex (16% of societies), with female infanticide more common than male infanticide.

Infanticide is usually viewed by social scientists as a form of birth control used to limit the size of the population when food supplies are uncertain or when the care of existing children will be hampered by the presence of additional children (Langer, 1974; Granzberg, 1973). Female infanticide has drawn special attention as a form of population control, particularly in polygynous societies as a means of balancing the sex ratio.

Childhood

As shown in Table 2.1, children around the world are at risk from a wide variety of types of family violence, generally carried out by their parents or with their parents' tacit approval. However, as with violence directed at infants, most types of violence directed at children tend to occur in only a few societies. In fact, the only types with widespread distribution are the use of physical punishment in child rearing and fighting between siblings.

As a background to discussing physical punishment, it is important to review the full range of child-rearing techniques used around the world. Barry et al. (1980) supply the relevant data, based on the Standard Cross-Cultural Sample. (The Standard Cross-Cultural Sample is a sample of 186 societies presumably representative of all societal types.) Barry and his associates distinguish among three categories of child-rearing techniques—exhorting, rewarding, and punishing. Exhorting includes expecting children to follow the example set by adults, public pressure, verbal commands, lecturing, and moralizing. Setting an example is the most-used exhorting technique for both boys and girls and younger and older children, occurring in about 82% of societies. Lecturing is also common, occurring in about 72% of societies.

The second category of child-rearing techniques—rewarding—covers the use of ceremonies to reward specific achievements, such as earning good grades in school or to honor the child as an individual through ceremonies such as birthday parties. Rewarding also includes gift giving either in the form of material objects or the conferring of special privileges. Gift giving is a widespread technique with young children, with ceremonies more important with older children.

Punishment is the third category of child-rearing techniques and includes teasing to shame or ridicule the child, scolding, threatening, and physical punishment meant to inflict pain. Physical punishment is the second most-used technique for both boys and girls and younger and older children. It is used by parents and other caretakers in about 77% of the societies in the Standard Cross-Cultural Sample. In our 90-society sample I find a similar pattern, with physical punishment of children including slapping, spanking, hitting, beating, scalding, burning, pushing, pinching, and switching present in 74% of the societies.

While physical punishment of children is widespread among the cultures of the world, its actual frequency of use varies widely from one society to another. I found that physical punishment is regularly used in only 13.3% of the 90 societies, frequently used in 21.1%, infrequently used in 40% and rarely or never used in 26.5%. In addition, as the data cited here suggest, many techniques other than punishment are also used, both apart from or in conjunction with actual punishment. The Burusho (Hunza) of Pakistan are typical of a large number of societies in the manner in which adults use physical punishment:

> The Hunzukuts are kind to their kiddies and fond of them, but have happily no time to spoil them, and as the children have always something new and interesting to do they are very rarely troublesome. If they are, some grown-up will give them a mild smack on the head (the little cap prevents its hurting much) and all is well again [Lorimer, 1939: 137].

In order not to give the impression that all societies eschew the use of physical punishment, consider the Goajiro of Colombia who rely on physical punishment more than any other society I encountered:

> There are punishments of various kinds. Some are corporal and consist of striking the child, and these are the most frequent. They slap them on the mouth when they are insolent when given an order or when they give a sharp answer to the father or mother. They are punched and kicked or are whipped with lassos or riding whips, with twigs from woods or cudgels; but the mother generally beats them with a bunch of nettles when they commit any kind of naughtiness. . . . Another quite common form of punishment is to take the child and put him into a mesh bag of agave fiber, sling it on one of the high branches on an enramada [bough-covered shelter] and rotate it until the child is nauseated and vomits, becoming unconscious. He is then lowered and left on the ground until he recovers [Gutierrez de Pineda, 1950: 32-33].

The Goajiro aside, the majority of societies do not rely on physical punishment as their major child-rearing technique. Rather, as the data from Barry et al. (1980) suggest, most parents around the world rely on a variety of techniques, with physical punishment most often used to stop current misbehavior rather than to inculcate specific behaviors or values. Setting an example, rewarding through gifts and ceremonies, and lecturing are often far more important than is physical punishment in shaping behavior and values.

Fighting between siblings is the second type of family violence directed at children of interest to us here. Our data suggest that violence between siblings is not especially common in societies around the world. It is reported as present in only 43.7% of the societies in our sample. However, since I could find information on sibling violence for only 48 of the 90 societies in the sample, there is some question as to whether sibling violence is underreported because it is often overlooked by ethnographers (perhaps because it is so common in Western societies) or whether sibling violence is not mentioned because it does not occur. My inclination is to assume that sibling violence is underreported in the ethnographic literature and thus actually does occur more frequently than the 43.7% figure suggests. But, as this is an unproven assumption, I will rely on the data at hand and use the 43.7% figure throughout the book.

Sibling violence may be relatively infrequent in non-Western societies for two reasons. First, in some societies siblings are segregated by age, and in many societies by sex. Thus the opportunity for violence between older and younger siblings or brothers and sisters, so common in American society, is considerably reduced. Second, in many societies, older siblings play a central role in helping care for their younger brothers and sisters. In this role, they often follow the lead of their parents or other adults in the child-rearing techniques they use. Since, in many societies physical punishment is used infrequently and is less important than other techniques, it follows that sibling caretakers will tend not to punish physically siblings in their care.

Adolescence

Discussing family violence directed at adolescents poses two problems. The first is that the concept of adolescence as a distinct developmental stage in the life cycle is difficult to apply cross-culturally. In some societies, like our own, adolescence is a long, drawn-out stage with a clear beginning and somewhat less clear end-point. But, in other societies there is no comparable stage, with children passing directly from the status of child to that of adult, sometimes with and sometimes without the benefit of a formal ceremony marking the transition. Thus, for the purposes of discussion here, adolescence is equated with the life stage, regardless of physical maturity, during which the child is seen by members of his or her society as preparing for or passing into adulthood.

The second problem is deciding whether or not to categorize pain inflicted on adolescents during initiation ceremonies as a form of family violence. Initiation ceremonies are a formal social recognition that the child is passing into the next stage in the life cycle, either adolescence or adulthood, and often, though not always, occur at or after the biological changes associated with puberty. Initiation ceremonies occur in about 55% of societies, with more societies having ceremonies for girls than for boys (Barry and Schlegel, 1980). Both our data and Barry and Schlegel's indicate that painful procedures or pain inflicted during genital operations occur in about 47% of the societies with ceremonies. Painful procedures include scarification, tattooing, tooth extraction, and the like to change the child's appearance; and whippings, cold baths, forced starvation, and the like as part of the ceremony or training program leading up to the ceremony. Genital operations, generally conducted without anesthesia, include circumcision and subincision for boys and clitoridectomy for girls. These procedures as well as the ceremony in general are carried out by adults in the community, with the support of the child's immediate family, but usually without their active participation. Thus pain infliction during initiation ceremonies is violence directed at children or adolescents by adults with the approval of the child's family. Does this constitute family violence? Some would say no, arguing that the parents have no choice, as their child can become an adult member of society only by completing the ceremony. In addition, they might argue that the parents, having experienced the ceremony themselves, suffer along with their children. Following the behavioral conceptualization of family violence set forth in Chapter 1, I argue that pain infliction during initiation ceremonies is a form of family violence because it is condoned by the parents and carried out by their agents. That some societies choose to use pain to help turn children into adults while others do not is an important cross-cultural variation that must be considered in any analysis of both violence in general and family violence in particular. This point is elaborated on in Chapter 5 in which I discuss the strong link between pain infliction on female adolescents and wife beating.

Adulthood

As Table 2.1 suggests, much family violence is directed at adult family members. Husbands beat their wives, wives beat their husbands, children beat their parents, in polygynous societies co-wives beat each other, and in matrilocal societies brothers beat their sisters.

Wife beating is the most common form of family violence around the world. It occurs at least occasionally in 84.5% of the societies in our sample. It occurs in virtually all households in 18.8% of societies, in a majority of households in 29.9%, in a minority of households in 37.8%, and never or very rarely in 15.5%. Wife beatings severe enough to kill or permanently injure the wife are reported in 46.6% of all societies in the sample—that is, in 58% of societies in which wife beating is present. As wife beating is discussed in more detail in the following section, we can skip ahead to some less common forms of adult family violence— husband beating, fighting between co-wives, and sister beating—before looking at wife beating in more detail.

Husband beating occurs in 26.9% of the societies in our sample, or in about a third of the societies with wife beating. In about 6.7% of societies husband beating occurs in a majority of households, and in a minority of households in the other 20.2%. Husband beating occurs only in societies in which wife beating also occurs. Not only is husband beating less common cross-culturally, but, in general, it occurs less often than does wife beating in those societies in which both are present. The Toradja of the Celebes are a good example of this pattern (Adriani and Kruzt, 1951: 323):

> The rule is that beating is permitted whenever one of the parties is "guilty." . . . If we consider what the Toradja calls *sala*, "guilt," in the domestic sense of the word, however, then the husband gets off easily. A husband beats his wife because he had to wait too long for his meal; because of this the wife was "guilty"; but no Toradja would think of declaring the husband "guilty" if he comes home long after mealtime, or simply stays to eat with someone else.

However, in some societies with wife beating, there are circumstances that empower the wife to beat her husband, with evidence of adultery being the most common. Among the Tikopia of Polynesia, for example, a husband who stays out all night is greeted by a stick-wielding wife who beats him on the legs and pinches him to draw blood, a punishment he must endure in silence for fear of awakening the other residents of the household (Firth, 1936: 133).

Alice Schlegel (1972) has brought to our attention the practice of adult brothers beating their adult sisters in societies with matrilineal descent systems. Schlegel categorizes the societies in her sample in terms of the degree of control brothers or husbands exert over their sisters or wives. In societies in which brothers dominate, sister beating is tolerated, but husband beating is not. Where husbands dominate, both wife beating and sister beating are tolerated, although wife beating is more common. In societies in which brothers and husbands share control, wife/sister beating is uncommon. The following account of a wife beating incident among the Trukese of the Caroline Islands indicates just how precarious a position a woman can be in when faced with the authority of her husband, which is reinforced by her brothers' support for the husband (Swartz, 1958: 472):

> One morning I heard a young man shouting at his wife that she had lost the key to the locked box she shared with him. . . . As I approached the house, the woman rushed out carrying her infant daughter and followed by her husband, who was brandishing a machete. He shouted "You are very disobedient," and struck her across the chest with the flat of the machete. The woman staggered back and began to wail that the baby had been cut. Her brother, who was with me, ran to her and began shaking her. "See the price of your disobedience!" he told her.

Fighting between co-wives in polygynous societies is another form of family violence largely unknown in the Western world. Co-wives are, of course, women who share the same husband and who often live in the same family compound or dwelling with the husband and their children. While there is some question about whether co-wives are kin to one another, there is little doubt that in most societies with polygynous marriage, co-wives are all members of the same residential family unit. That violence between co-wives will occasionally break-out is not surprising given the role complexity in polygynous family households. Not only are there two or more co-wives who share the same husband and must cooperate in economic matters, but there are their children who share the same father and are related to one another as half siblings. Thus there are often conflicts over sexual access to the husband, distribution of wealth, and disciplining of the children. Among the Siriono of Bolivia, for example, older wives sometimes fight with younger wives over sexual access to the husband (Holmberg, 1950: 50). However, aggression is not always directed at the other co-wife, as among the Kapauku of New Guinea, where sexual neglect might lead a wife to either attack another co-wife or destroy her husband's garden (Pospisil, 1958: 136).

One of the more troubling features of fighting between co-wives is that it appears to be part of a more general pattern of women in polygynous societies settling disputes through violence. Our data suggest that physical aggression between women occurs almost exclusively in societies with polygynous marriage, with much of it motivated by sexual jealousy, not just between co-wives but between women in general.

The other forms of family violence listed in Table 2.1 are sparsely distributed around the world, either because they occur in only a few societies (raiding for brides, for example), or because, while they do occur in many societies, they occur very rarely (matricide, for example).

Old Age

Widespread interest in family violence began in the early 1960s with interest in child abuse. By the mid-1970s, interest had spread to include spouse abuse, especially wife abuse. Now, in the 1980s, elder abuse has become a major focus of attention (Pillemer and Wolf, 1986). Cross-cultural studies of the treatment of the aged are limited both in quantity and quality (Levinson and Malone, 1980). Perhaps the most reliable data come from Glascock's (Glascock and Wagner, 1986) study of the treatment of the aged in 60 societies. Their data largely put to rest the popular notion that the elderly are routinely left behind to die in small-scale societies. While this does occur in some societies, it seems confined mainly to a few nomadic groups and the practice is used only for those elderly who are too ill or weak to travel with the group. The elderly in most small-scale societies are treated with respect and cared for by their families and the community. However, there are exceptions to this pattern: in 12% of societies some elderly people are thought to be witches; in 12% of societies the elderly must give up their property; in 21% some elderly are not allowed to live with the main social group; and in 21% some elderly are killed because they are old. These percentages aside, the key point is that the elderly are respected, cared for, and afforded special privileges in many societies, perhaps because they are the repositories of vital information or resources of interest to the younger members of society (Simmons, 1945; Maxwell and Silverman, 1970).

WIFE BEATING

As mentioned here, wife beating occurs in more societies around the world than any other type of family violence. For the most part, wife beating has been conceptualized as a unidimensional phenomenon by most social and behavioral scientists working in the family violence field. Gelles and Straus's (1979) suggestion that family violence might be conceptualized profitably along legitimate-illegitimate and expressive instrumental continuums has largely been ignored. The few formal attempts to develop a typology of wife-beating types have focused on frequency and severity of wife-beating events (Bowker, 1983).

By contrast, my research suggests that wife beating might be a multidimensional phenomenon, with at least three different types of wife beating existing around the world. This three-tier typology is based on the primary reason that wife beating occurs in a society. By reason I do not mean cause, in the theoretical sense, but the reason the people in a specific society *believe* that wife beating occurs in their society. An analysis of the data on wife beating for the 90-society sample suggests that people around the world believe that wife beating occurs or should occur for three main reasons. First, people in 17 societies believe that wife beating occurs primarily as a punishment for adultery or because the husband suspects that his wife has been unfaithful. Nine of these societies are American Indian groups in North and South America, with the Arapaho fairly typical:

> Occasionally a suspicious man calmly sent his wife away, either to her paramour or to her home. More often he became angry and jealous. Usually he whipped her, and cut off the tip of her nose or her braids, or both. According to Kroeber (1902, p. 13), he also slashed her cheeks. This treatment of an unfaithful wife was conventional and neither her parents nor the tribe did anything about it [Hilger, 1952: 212].

Thus in these societies, I categorize wife beating as sexual jealousy beating, since it occurs primarily in response to real or suspected adultery by the wife.

The second type of wife beating I call wife beating for cause; that is, people in 15 societies believe that a husband may beat his wife, so long as he has a good reason. What constitutes a good reason is commonly understood by men and women alike and often involves the wife's failure to perform her duties or to treat her husband with the degree of respect he expects. The Trukese are typical:

> Wife beating is quite common but is appropriate only if there is a good "reason." When a woman violates the proscriptions on "haughty behavior" or is disobedient, her husband may beat her with no fear of interference from her relatives. However, if a husband beats his wife too frequently, or if the beatings are too severe, the woman's relatives will "pity her" and will cause a separation [Swartz, 1958: 472].

The third type of wife beating is wife beating at will, since people in the 39 societies in which this type predominates believe that it is the husband's right to beat his wife for any reason or for no reason at all. This is by far the most common type of wife beating, and a number of major features are displayed by the Serbs of Yugoslavia:

> The peasants consider, and so do their wives, that this is the husband's right as head of the family. If a woman does anything wrong and the husband does not give her a good beating, she begins to despise him, counts him a weakling and strives to assume his place in the home. . . . In the opinion of the village, the husband is absolute master in the home, who must see that there is order in the home, who has the right to punish the members of the family if they do anything very wrong [Erlich, 1966: 270].

Table 2.2 provides some information about the differences between these three types of wife beating. The three types are compared for three descriptive factors and two theoretical factors. The descriptive factors are frequency of wife beating, severity of wife beating, and intervention by outsiders in wife beating incidents, with higher scores indicating more frequent or severe beating and less outside intervention. The theoretical factors are the degree to which men solve disputes peacefully or violently and male dominance in the household, with higher scores indicating violent resolutions and male dominance. Both of these factors have been shown to be strong predictors of wife beating frequency (see Chapters 3 and 5). The means displayed in the table indicate that there are some significant differences between types on the descriptive factors, with sexual jealousy beatings tending to be more severe and beatings at will occurring more often and being less subject to outside intervention. However, there are no significant differences on the theoretical factors, suggesting that for theory-testing purposes, wife beating can be treated as a unidimensional phenomenon.

Before moving on to our analysis of the relationships between different types of family violence, we need to consider one other type of wife beating—wife beating that occurs mainly when the husband is consuming or has recently consumed alcoholic beverages. A number of studies suggest that alcohol use may be directly or indirectly related to family violence (especially wife beating) in American families. However, many of these studies are dated or methodologically unsophisticated and leave "Questions of how, how much, when, and why . . . largely unanswered" (Morgan, 1982: 246; Epstein et al., 1978). In the sample I found seven societies in which wife beating occurs mainly in association with alcohol consumption by the husband, one society in which it occurs usually when both the husband and wife are drinking, and five societies in which both alcohol- and nonalcohol-related wife beating are reported. In all other societies, alcohol use apparently plays no or only a limited role in wife beating.

The Tzeltal of Mexico are a good example of the seven societies with what might be called institutionalized alcohol-related wife beating (Metzger, 1964). Physical aggression is a rather common occurrence between drunk Tzeltal men at the frequent fiestas. So too, is male aggression directed at their wives. In fact, it is so common that it is specifically proscribed in the wedding ceremony: "You, boy, esteem your wife, don't scold her, don't strike her. When you drink aguardiente, ask for your supper as one ought to, ask for your pozole as one ought to" (Metzger, 1964: 82). Unfortunately, the proscription is generally ignored and the wife excuses her husband's behavior with comments such as, "I will pardon you, but I am ashamed of you." "Maybe he's

TABLE 2.2
Types of Wife Beating

Wife Beating Type	Frequency (1-4)	Severity (1-4)	Intervention (1-6)	Dispute Resolution (1-3)	Male Dominance (1-3)
I (adultery)	2.53	3.82	2.00	1.75	2.13
II (reason)	2.53	2.89	2.54	1.43	2.62
III (at will)	3.05	3.29	3.21	1.79	2.35

crazy." "That's just the way he is." The husband, for his part, asks for forgiveness on the grounds that "I don't remember what I did" or "I won't do it again."

Based on the data at hand, it seems that alcohol use is of little or no importance in family violence events in most societies around the world. At the same time, however, there are a few societies, such as the Tzeltal, in which alcohol use is a key component in the sequence of events leading up to wife-beating incidents, with the supposed disinhibiting effects of alcohol used to excuse behavior that would not otherwise be tolerated by the wife, her family, or the community.

PATTERNS OF FAMILY VIOLENCE

Ever since interest in family violence began in the early 1960s, researchers, clinicians, and policymakers have been intrigued with the idea that family violence may be transferred from one generation to the next within families. Most of the thinking has taken either a learning theory or social milieu perspective, based on the assumption that adults who themselves were victims of or witnessed violence in their childhood homes are more likely than those without such a background to act violently toward their spouses or children. The empirical evidence bearing on the intergenerational hypothesis is mixed: Some studies support the basic proposition (Silvers, 1969; Freedman, 1975; Oliver and Taylor, 1971; Herrenkohl et al., 1983; Stacey and Shupe, 1983), while other researchers and reviewers (Straus, 1983; Jayaratne, 1977; Pagelow, 1981) suggest that intergenerational transmission is not an especially powerful predictor of family violence.

Related to the intergenerational hypothesis is the broader notion that any specific type of family violence, such as wife beating or infanticide, is but one part of a broader pattern of violence in a society. One could reasonably assume that such a societal pattern of violence would be

TABLE 2.3
Relationships Among Types of Family Violence

	(1)	(2)	(3)	(4)	(5)
(1) wife beating		.322*	.249	.317*	.387*
(2) child punishment			.483*	−.053	.044
(3) sibling aggression				.191	.155
(4) husband beating					.313*
(5) infanticide					

*Significant at .05 level.

reflected in family relationships characterized by violence. This idea is explored further in Chapter 3, but bears directly on the data summarized in Table 2.3. The coefficients reported in the table suggest that there is a general though not especially powerful pattern of relationships among five common types of family violence.

It is interesting that the strongest relationship is between infanticide and husband beating, a pattern that defies explanation based on any of the theoretical perspectives outlined in Chapter 1. The correlations in Table 2.3 do not bear directly on the intergenerational transmission hypothesis, though they do provide indirect support for its validity. As mentioned in Chapter 1, the intergenerational hypothesis suggests that individuals who themselves were victims of or witnesses to family violence in their families of orientation are more likely to become involved in violent family relations in their families of procreation than are individuals without the same violence-laden development background. As the hypothesis focuses on the individual at two points in time, it cannot be tested with the societal-level, synchronic data used here. However, if the intergenerational hypothesis were entirely without merit, we would expect to find no relationships between these five types of family violence at the societal level. That there are statistical relationships among some of the variables suggests that there may well be both a cultural patterning of family violence (different types of violence cooccuring in single societies) as well as a cyclical pattern of intergenerational transmission in families in those societies.

SUMMARY

In this chapter, I have reviewed the cross-cultural distribution of family violence. There are dozens of different types of family violence around the world, ranging from the very common wife beating to rare types, such as raiding for wives or the sacrifice of children. While family members at all stages in the life cycle are at risk, adults, and especially adult women, are at greatest risk. These types of family violence exhibit a wide range of frequency, both across and within societies. Wife beating, the most common type of family violence around the world, seems to come in three basic forms—beatings over sexual jealousy, beatings for cause, and beatings at will. While these three types vary in severity and frequency across societies, it seems likely that the same basic forces cause all three. Finally, there is some patterning of family violence within societies, with the presence of one form of family violence an indicator that other forms are present as well.

-3-

FAMILY VIOLENCE AND OTHER TYPES OF VIOLENCE

With this chapter we begin our search for the causes of family violence in societies around the world. Our focus here is on the two most common types of family violence—wife beating and the physical punishment of children. The idea that the frequency or severity of family violence might be related to the frequency or severity of other types of violence in a society pervades much of the current thinking about the causes of family violence. It also influences policies and programs designed to control family violence. Thus it is fitting that we begin our search for causes by examining the relationship between family violence and other forms of violence.

Violence is a complex subject and violent behavior can be defined and categorized in a variety of ways. We can distinguish between violence usually carried out by individuals (assault or suicide) and violence carried out by groups (war or riots). Or we can categorize violence as either internal (directed at members of one's own society) or external (directed at members of other societies). And we can distinguish between direct violence aimed at some appropriate target and indirect violence aimed at an inappropriate target. Because of the multifaceted nature of violent behavior, and because we are interested in explaining family violence in the context of societal violence in general, it is important to begin with a clear definition of violence and a clear classification scheme for the types of violence I will be concerned with. Violence is defined here as an action of one or more individuals that is meant to cause physical pain to one or more other individuals or nonhuman animals, or to destroy material property. Violence is categorized in terms of the relationship between the aggressor and the intended target of the violent act: (1) household members; (2) acquaintances; (3) strangers. As defined in Chapter 1, household members are individuals with whom the aggressor shares a dwelling. Acquaintances are individuals who live in the same community as the aggressor and who, it is reasonable to assume, the aggressor has some personal knowledge of. Business partners, relatives residing in different households, and other residents of the community are all categorized as acquaintances. Strangers are individuals the aggressor does not have personal knowledge of because they come from another community in a heavily populated society or from a different society. Violence directed at nonhuman animals such as dogs or at physical objects is also categorized as stranger violence.

I need to cover a lot of ground in this chapter. I begin with a review of general theories of violence that predict a relationship between family violence and other forms of violence. In the second section I present the results of an analysis of the relationship between wife beating and child punishment and other forms of violence. The third and fourth sections provide more detailed analyses of two relationships noted in the second section—those between wife beating and painful female initiation ceremonies and wife beating and conflict resolution. In the fifth and final section, I shift the focus and discuss wife beating as a cause of rather than as the result of other forms of violence.

THE CULTURAL PATTERNING OF VIOLENCE

Much of the recent cross-cultural research on human violence has been based on one or the other of two basic, though conflicting, models of human aggression (Levinson and Malone, 1980). The first model, the drive discharge or catharsis model suggests that all groups have an innate level of aggression that must be periodically discharged in some way (Sipes, 1973). The second model, the culture pattern model (which incorporates a social learning perspective), suggests that some societies have a basic set of values and beliefs that emphasize aggression and violence. In these societies, as compared to other societies that lack such an orientation, violence is likely to be found in all or many spheres of activity including interpersonal relationships, family life, child rearing, religious ceremonies, warfare, and games and sports. Taken to its extreme, the culture pattern approach suggests that in some societies violence is a "way of life."

Research on family violence has followed both the catharsis and culture pattern models. However, since the catharsis model has been applied primarily at the family or interactional level, it is beyond the scope of our investigation here. For example, the finding that wife beating and child abuse occur more frequently in households in which the husband/father is unemployed rests on the proposition that unemployment leads to frustration, stress, and rage that reaches a point at which it must be discharged. The wife or children are a convenient and easy though inappropriate target for that rage. While it would be useful to test this idea cross-culturally, the data at hand are simply not focused or detailed enough to enable me to do so. Thus the focus must shift to explanations for family violence that rest on the culture pattern model, as some of these hypotheses can be tested with the data at hand.

Five hypotheses derived from the general culture pattern model have been used to explain family violence. The first, the subculture of violence hypothesis, suggests that violence is a learned behavior pattern that is shared by members of groups whose value systems encourage the use of violence (Wolfgang and Ferracuti, 1967). While not widely used in family violence research yet, the hypothesis does provide a theoretical basis for what has been called the "macho male hypothesis" of family violence. For example, Bowker (1983) reports that male social embeddedness, as indicated by frequent contact with male friends, is related to more frequent and more severe wife beating, child abuse, beating of pregnant wives, and a longer duration (in years) of wife beatings in his sample of Milwaukee families. Interpretation of Bowker's findings in the context of the subculture of violence hypothesis suggests that wife beating and child abuse may be the result of a male subculture of peers whose value system justifies or perhaps even encourages the use of physical violence against one's wife.

The second culture pattern hypothesis, the cultural consistency hypothesis, suggests that cultural values that are, on the surface, seemingly unrelated to family violence may, in fact, actually create norms governing family life that both lead to and perpetuate violence between family members. Carroll (1980) contrasts family relations among Mexican-Americans and Jewish-Americans to demonstrate the applicability of the cultural consistency hypothesis. Mexican-Americans have a value system that emphasizes male dominance, age dominance, and strict discipline. This system leads to norms that emphasize coercive power, and causes sons to fear and to feel distant from their fathers. This combination of values and norms leads to violence in parent-child relations, a pattern that is often transferred from generation to generation.

Jewish-Americans, on the other hand, have a value system that emphasizes the pursuit of knowledge, male religiosity, Jewish identity, and parent-child involvement. The resulting norms reinforce compassion for children, intellectuality, and verbal dexterity. This combination leads to nonviolent family relationships. Carroll's cultural consistency hypothesis is an important contribution to the search for causes of family violence as it provides a framework for the analysis of relationships among beliefs, values, norms, behavior, and the structuring of social relationships. However, the cultural consistency hypothesis also runs the risk of "blaming" family violence on the culture, without full consideration of environmental and historical factors and processes.

The third variant of the culture pattern model is the well known "family socialization into violence hypothesis" discussed at the close of Chapter 2. The family socialization hypothesis suggests that violence between family members is passed on from one generation to the next by individuals who were victims of or who witnessed family violence in their childhood homes. Although there is still some disagreement over the question of women "learning" to be victims, most researchers would be comfortable with Straus's (1983: 217) conclusion that: "The idea that child-abusing parents were themselves victims of abuse, and that wife-beating husbands come from violent families, is now widely accepted." Of course, since the family socialization hypothesis is operationalized at the family level, it cannot be directly tested with the cross-cultural data available to us here. However, as suggested in Chapter 2, our finding that different forms of family violence are associated with one another does provide indirect support for the hypothesis.

The fourth approach is the cultural spillover hypothesis that suggests that "the more a society tends to endorse the use of physical force to attain socially approved ends (such as order in the schools, crime control, and international dominance), the greater the likelihood that this legitimization of force will be generalized to other spheres of life where force is less socially approved, such as the family and relations between the sexes" (Baron and Straus, 1983: 217). The cultural spillover hypothesis has drawn support from Straus and Baron's (1985) study of legitimate violence and illegitimate violence (rape frequency) in the United States, Sanday's (1981) cross cultural comparative study linking rape to warfare, Archer and Gardner's (1984) cross-national study tying warfare to homicide rates, and Minturn et al.'s (1969) finding that rape is more common in societies in which pubescent boys are subjected to genital mutilations such as circumcision and subincision.

The fifth and final culture pattern hypothesis is really the full-blown culture pattern theory itself. The culture pattern model suggests that societies exhibit either many forms of violence or few forms (Russell, 1972; Sipes, 1973). That is, they are usually generally aggressive or generally peaceful. Of the many cross-cultural studies of the culture pattern model (see Levinson and Malone, 1980, or Naroll, 1983 for reviews) two bear directly on the relationship between wife beating and other forms of violence. Unfortunately, they produce somewhat conflicting results. Working with a sample of 86 societies, and using rigorous comparative methodological techniques, Masamura (1979) found wife beating associated with high rates of personal crime, theft, aggression, suicide, homicide, feuding, and warfare. Lester (1980), in a far less careful study, found wife beating associated with cruel treatment of war captives, mutilation of children, and drunken brawling, but unrelated to homicide, suicide, and warfare frequency.

Beyond these two studies is a substantial body of cross-cultural research that suggests a relationship between various forms of violence such as warfare, displaced aggression, and the use of aggressive medical therapies, and a heightened concern with aggression in child rearing (Whiting and Child, 1953; Kiev, 1960; Prothro, 1960; Russell, 1972). And there is a related body of cross-cultural studies that have consistently shown a relationship between a belief in malevolent, punishing spirits and the physical punishment of children (Lambert et al., 1959; Spiro and D'Andrade, 1958; Whiting, 1967; Otterbein and Otterbein, 1973; Prescott, 1975; Rohner, 1975). Finally, it is worth noting Hanmer and Saunder's (1984) public-private perpetuation model of violence against women. Their formulation suggests that fear of attacks by strangers forces women to become dependent on men whom they know, which makes it easier for those men to assault them, a pattern that is then reinforced by the reluctance of police to intervene in domestic violence situations. Thus there is some support from cross-cultural research for the proposition that family violence will be more common in societies in which other forms of violence are also common.

Having completed this brief overview of theoretical approaches derived from the general culture pattern of violence model, I can now move on to the results of direct tests of the cultural spillover and general culture pattern hypotheses and an indirect test of the family socialization hypotheses.

FAMILY VIOLENCE AND THE PATTERNING OF VIOLENCE

The basic results of the analysis are summarized in Table 3.1.

These results offer little support for the spillover hypothesis and partial support for the culture pattern hypothesis. As you will recall, the spillover hypothesis posits a relationship between legitimate violence and illegitimate violence or violence that may be something less than socially acceptable. I am assuming here that wife beating and physical punishment of children are somewhat less socially approved than are some of the other types of violence listed in Table 3.1. Of course, this assumption is not entirely valid as there are societies in our sample in which family violence is considered legitimate, or, as I noted in Chapter 2, legitimate in certain contexts or within certain limits. This assumption about what is legitimate or illegitimate violence is the crucial weakness of the spillover hypothesis, as in many social groups it is often impossible to distinguish empirically legitimate from illegitimate violence. Keeping the limits of this assumption in mind, we would expect, if

TABLE 3.1
Family Violence and Other Types of Violence

	Wife Beating	Child Punishment
Household members		
wife beating	———	.322*
husband beating	.317*	−.053
child punishment	.322*	———
infanticide	.387*	.044
sibling aggression	.249	.483*
Acquaintances		
punishment of criminals	.079*	.247*
female initiation pain	.483*	.363*
initiation pain	−.001	−.162
female fighting	.252*	−.195
male fighting	.341*	−.036
drunken brawling	.128	.034
Strangers		
animal cruelty	−.013	−.226*
torture of the enemy	−.050	−.217
warfare ethos	.148	−.121
warfare goal	.194	−.064

*Significant at .05 level.

the spillover hypothesis were correct, to find both wife beating and the physical punishment of children associated with an ethos emphasizing warfare, pursuit of military glory, regular torture of captured enemy warriors, cruel treatment of domestic animals, physical punishment of criminals, and painful initiation ceremonies for adolescents. The results show that of these seven variables, only pain in initiation ceremonies for girls strongly predicts both wife beating and child punishment. Thus the spillover hypothesis in its general form can be rejected as an explanation for family violence at least in a universal or cross-cultural sense. However, it cannot be rejected entirely, since we still must consider the strong relationship between pain infliction in initiation ceremonies for girls and wife beating and the somewhat weaker relationship with child punishment. I return to this matter in greater detail in the next section.

The correlation coefficients in Table 3.1 provide partial support for the culture pattern hypothesis. Neither wife beating nor child punishment is related to external violence—warfare ethos, pursuit of military glory, or torturing of enemy captives. Nor are they related to cruel treatment of domestic animals. However, wife beating is strongly related to three of the six forms of acquaintance violence and child punishment to pain in female initiation ceremonies and the physical punishment of criminals. Thus these findings suggest that wife beating is part of a broader culture pattern of violent relationships between persons who reside in the same community. We can expect to find more wife beating in communities where men brawl with one another when drunk, where women fight with other women, where men fight with other men, and where girls are subjected to painful initiation ceremonies. The most interesting relationships here are those between wife beating and male and female fighting that suggest that wife beating may be part of a pattern of adult conflict resolution through violence, a point discussed in more detail later.

Although not displayed in the table, the findings also suggest that the severity of wife beating incidents is consistently related to the presence of violence in a society. Women are more likely to be permanently injured, scarred, or even killed by their husbands in societies in which animals are treated cruelly, criminals are subjected to physical punishments, enemy captives are tortured, men and women solve conflicts violently, girls are subjected to painful initiation ceremonies, and military glory is a source of male pride.

Child punishment, on the other hand, seems to exist outside any general pattern of violence in the community or the society. This may be owing in part to the often random manner in which physical punishment is used by parents and other caretakers. In many of the societies in our sample, physical punishment is not seen as a regular component of the arsenal of child-rearing techniques available to parents. Rather, it is often used sporadically, in fits of parental rage or frustration.

The final culture pattern model hypothesis of interest here is the family socialization through violence hypothesis indirectly tested through the correlations pertaining to violence among household members. While the coefficients say nothing about the intergeneration transfer of violence in the family, they do suggest that, at least at a given point in time, if one form of violence occurs in a household, so too will other forms.

PAINFUL INITIATION CEREMONIES FOR GIRLS AND WIFE BEATING

It is important to keep in mind here that initiation ceremonies do not occur in all societies, nor is pain a part of the ceremony in all societies in which ceremonies do occur. Further, there is a clear regional pattern to the distribution of painful female ceremonies around the world, with such ceremonies occurring primarily in societies in North and South

America and Oceania. The link between painful ceremonies for girls and wife beating frequency makes sense when we remember that one key function of initiation ceremonies is to prepare children or adolescents for the adult role they are about to assume. Thus the ceremony and the activities associated with it are designed to introduce the initiate to her new adult role and status and teach her the skills and knowledge required of her in that new role. When viewed in this framework, it seems obvious why painful initiation ceremonies for girls occur so often in societies with frequent wife beating. Wife beating, whether accepted by all members of the society or not, is a fact of married life and the painful ceremony is one means of alerting the girl to and preparing her for the physical pain she will likely experience at the hands of her husband. Thus socially sanctioned violence during the ceremony prepares the girl for the violence she will experience in marriage. I might extend this line of reasoning one step further and argue that violence during the ceremony also encourages subsequent wife beatings, as both the wife and husband enter marriage expecting beatings to be a part of the relationship.

Your may recall that in Chapter 2, I identified the Goajiro of Columbia as a society in which parents use particularly cruel methods to discipline their children. Not surprisingly, Goajiro husbands also regularly beat their wives. In fact, the husband doesn't just beat his wife, but also brags about it; if he thinks he can avoid retribution by her family, he might even kill her. Goajiro female initiation ceremonies fit right in with this pattern of violence and provide a real-life example of the correlational pattern shown in Table 3.1 (Gutierrez de Pineda, 1950). At her first menstruation, the girl is given a drink to make her vomit. Her head is then shaved and she is suspended in a hammock from the roof of the house for three to five days. During this time she receives no food or water and is forbidden to change her position. When she is lowered from the hammock she is fed, bathed, and secluded from men in a separate room where her training in domestic duties begins. During this training period of 1 to 12 months she is taught how to cook, how to keep house, how to greet guests in her home, her wifely duties, her legal obligations to her husband and his family, and the history of the Goajiro. This seclusion ends with a communal feast and celebration of her new role and status in the community. One of the functions of this rigorous training is quite clear: "It is a system of preparation for adult social life, in the sense that, by its means, are acquired knowledge of proper cultural patterns" (Gutierrez de Pineda, 1950: 57). One of those patterns is family violence, and whether she or her family approve or not, she is prepared for it by the painful initiation process.

SPOUSAL VIOLENCE AS A FORM OF
CONFLICT RESOLUTION

There appears to be no end to the ways in which people around the world resolve or attempt to resolve interpersonal conflicts. To give some idea of the range of conflict management techniques used, I have listed some of the major ones used by societies in our sample in Table 3.2. The techniques listed in the table are categorized according to whether they involve violence or not and the type of violence (direct, indirect, or verbal). There are, of course, other ways to conceptualize conflict resolution. Koch et al. (1976), for example, distinguish between dyadic and triadic conflict management. In dyadic conflict management only the parties involved in the conflict situation are directly involved in its resolution, through coercion or negotiation. In triadic conflict management a third party is involved, either as a mediator or as an adjudicator.

While people in all societies rely on more than one conflict management technique, it seems clear from the data that in many societies some approaches are more widespread and considered more appropriate than others. For example, the Southern Ojibwa of Wisconsin freely resort to violence:

> Violence and waywardness are not peculiar to Ojibwa marriage. The impulse of the moment will cause a man to attack his mother, a son-in-law to crack open the head of his mother-in-law, a son to call the police on his father, one relative to send bad medicine to another, and what is worse, a man to accuse his brother of this openly [Landes, 1937: 84].

While Ojibwa violence is random and out-of-control, the Chukchee of Siberia (Sverdrup, 1938: 112) have a controlled, institutionalized form of violent conflict resolution in which the "law of the fist rules." An angry Chukchee accuses the alleged guilty party in a loud, screaming, insulting tirade. If the accused feels that he is right, he responds with an equally loud and insulting tirade of his own. The parties then grab each other and each attempts to throw the other to the ground. The one who winds up on the ground has his face rubbed in the snow, is beaten around the head and kicked until he gives in. The winner is considered to be "right" and "lights his pipe and hands it to his opponent, and all is well."

At the opposite extreme from the Obijwa and Chukchee are the Javanese:

> A common way of handling quarrels, customary among both children and adults, is the *satru* pattern—not speaking to each other. Children may *satru* with their playmates for several days, adult sisters for several years, and divorced couples or debtor and creditor *satru* for their entire lives....

TABLE 3.2
Conflict Management Techniques

Direct violence
    fighting
    homicide
    hair-pulling
    public duels
    competitive sports (wrestling)
    sorcery
    witchcraft

Indirect violence
    spiting
    destroy own property
    destroy another's property
    arson
    suicide
    hunting

Verbal aggression
    argue
    insults
    shouting matches
    swearing
    gossip
    word duels
    song duels

Nonviolent
    silence
    avoidance
    apology
    mediation
    theft
    litigation
    fines
    community intervention
    compensation
    drinking bouts
    withdrawal
    confession

A *satru* relationship is almost institutionalized; such a quarrel is labeled as such and is respected by all in contact with the quarrelers [Geertz, 1961: 117-118].

Somewhere between violent and peaceful resolution societies are those with a broad range of conflict management techniques at their disposal. Which technique is actually used depends on the relationship between the parties, the social context, and the cause of the quarrel. The Tarahumara, an Indian group in northern Mexico, use an interesting mix of violent and nonviolent techniques (Fried, 1952: 194-212). At the violent end, Tarahumara men might fight or even kill one another when drunk and men and young girls are reported to have committed suicide when faced with a seemingly unsolvable problem. Verbal confrontations are especially common and include hurling insults, arguing, scolding, spreading gossip, and accusing others of being witches or using sorcery to achieve their evil ends. Finally, the Tarahumara are not without nonviolent approaches, including sullen silence, desertion, moving to a new residence, mediation by native officials, or a trial before a government official.

Consideration of these various cultural patterns of conflict resolution is important as a way of providing a context for the following discussion of what seems to be the key relationship between family violence and other forms of violence in societies around the world. The coefficients in Table 3.3 suggest that wife beating and husband beating are associated with two other forms of violent conflict resolution—fighting between men to settle disputes and fighting between women to settle disputes. By fighting to settle disputes, I mean that people are more likely to use physical violence than either verbal aggression or nonviolent means to settle interpersonal conflicts. However, there is one important limitation to this pattern—since fighting between women occurs almost exclusively in societies with polygynous marriage, the general pattern does not hold for all societies.

Keeping this limitation in mind, it is nonetheless true that the pattern does occur in a variety of societies around the world, including the Mbuti Pygmy and Rundi of Africa, the Tamil of India, and the Bororo and Ona of South America. The Mbuti display all the key features and then some:

> The rules of self-help among the Mbuti are quite simple. It is perfectly proper to hit someone with anything wooden; it is not at all proper to draw blood, nor to hit anyone on the forehead, which is considered a dangerous spot [Turnbull, 1965: 188 190].

The Mbuti follow the rules closely: Women fight over borrowed cooking utensils, men over hunting territories; husbands beat their wives for domestic inadequacies and because of sexual jealousy, wives beat their husbands because they are poor hunters; old women break up domestic fights by beating both participants; brothers beat their sisters over the frustrations of daily life, and so on. Of course, most of these conflicts are short-lived and quickly forgotten, in accord with the general cultural pattern favoring the use of physical violence in the management of conflict.

TABLE 3.3
Relationships Among Types of Adult Violent Conflict

	(1)	(2)	(3)	(4)
(1) wife beating		.317*	.252*	.341*
(2) husband beating			.320*	.197
(3) female fighting				.375*
(4) male fighting				

*Significant at .05 level.

This association of spousal violence with other forms of violent interpersonal conflict resolution begs the question of why societies differ from one another in the types of conflict resolution techniques used. In other words, what causes some societies to use peaceful techniques and others to use violent ones? Unfortunately, there is little cross-cultural research on this question. The evidence does suggest, however, that a male sex identity conflict caused by a close mother-son relationship in childhood, widely believed to cause interpersonal violence, does not necessarily lead to hypermasculinity or to the use of violent techniques in adulthood (Koch et al., 1976; see Chapter 4, this volume). Similarly, Hickson (1986) reports that dependency in childhood is unrelated to the use of apology in dispute resolution. She does find, though, that the use of apology is more common in societies with a hierarchical social order. As already suggested, there is a pressing need for cross-cultural research that may suggest some causes of variation in conflict resolution techniques.

The idea that spousal violence can be understood as one part of a more general cultural pattern of violent conflict resolution has important implications for the control and prevention of family violence. This issue is discussed in detail in Chapter 7, but it is worth noting here that one important implication is that policies and programs aimed at preventing family violence cannot ignore the ways people resolve conflicts in the family, in the community, and in society.

FAMILY VIOLENCE AS A CAUSE OF OTHER TYPES OF VIOLENCE

So far, I have focused exclusively on family violence as a result of other types of violence or as part of a general pattern of violence. In this section, I shift the perspective to consider the possibility that family violence may directly cause other types of violence. We have already seen through the family-socialization-through-violence hypothesis that one form of family violence may lead to other forms. However, there is also a growing body of research that suggests that wife beating may lead directly to suicide or suicide attempts. Studies of battered women show a fairly high incidence of attempted suicides, with a recent review indicating that as many as 35% to 40% of battered women in the United States attempt suicide (Back et al., 1982; Pagelow, 1984; Stark and Flitcraft, 1985). Counts (in press) has recently extended this finding to the non-Western world through her own research among the Lusi-Kaliai of Papua New Guinea and a survey of the literature pertaining to other societies. A direct relationship between wife beatings or severe wife beating and subsequent suicide attempts by beaten wives is reported for the Kove of West New Britain, the Gainj and Maring of Papua New Guinea, the Fijians, and the Jivaro of Peru. Counts suggests that it may not be the beatings per se that lead wives to kill themselves, but beatings that are abusive and that bring shame to the woman. Obviously, the idea that wife beating or other forms of family violence might directly lead to other violence will be an important focus of future research.

SUMMARY

A variety of theoretical perspectives can be used to approach the question of whether family violence is part of a broader cultural pattern of violence. The data suggest that neither wife beating frequency nor the use of physical punishment in child rearing is part of any general pattern of violence, although severe wife beating is consistently associated with the regular use of violence. Wife beating is related to the use of painful initiation ceremonies for girls, a finding that suggests that the pain exists at least in part to prepare the girl for the pain she will suffer at the hands of her husband. The findings also suggest that both husband beating and wife beating exist in many societies as part of a broader pattern of violent interpersonal conflict resolution among adults in the community. This finding has especially significant implications for policy and program decisions about the control and prevention of family violence. Finally, I noted that an emerging body of research suggests that it might be fruitful to consider family violence as a cause of other types of violence, especially female suicide and suicide attempts.

-4-

SOCIAL STRUCTURE
AND FAMILY VIOLENCE

By social structure, I mean the norms, rules, and practices that govern the relationships between individuals and groups in a society. The number of people who live together, the nature of their relationships to one another, the rules that govern who may marry whom, the division of labor, status distinctions based on sex or age, and rules governing premarital sex are but a few of the elements of social structure present in all societies. When viewed cross-culturally, there is considerable variation among societies in the rules and practices that structure and guide social relations. For example, in the United States, the nuclear family composed of the husband/father, wife/mother, and their children is the preferred type of household unit. Among the Serbs of rural Yugoslavia, the extended family composed of two brothers, their wives and their children is the preferred household type. And among the Masai of Kenya, the polygynous family compound composed of the husband and his wives and children is the preferred form. This variation in social structure is precisely what makes the cross-cultural comparative method an especially powerful means for testing structural hypotheses about family violence. Only by comparing societies that vary on the structural dimension can we determine if structural factors influence the frequency and patterning of family violence. Over the last 10 to 15 years social structural theories have largely replaced or been combined with psychological ones to form the primary explanations for family violence. As outlined in Chapter 1, these include resource theory, exchange theory, ecological theory, social learning theory, and general systems theory (Rodman, 1972, Gelles, 1983, Garbarino, 1977). Embedded in these general theories are a number of hypotheses about the effect of various social structural factors on family violence. Five hypotheses can be deduced that are amenable to testing with the cross-cultural data available:

(1) Family violence will occur more often in societies in which social support networks within and between families are weak.

(2) Family violence will occur more often in societies in which child rearing practices are such that boys are likely to develop a sex identity conflict.

(3) Family violence will occur more often in societies with more complex socioeconomic systems.

(4) Family violence will occur more often in societies undergoing social change.

(5) Family violence will occur more often in societies in which men have more status and power than do women.

The fifth proposition—the sexual inequality hypothesis—has been afforded so much attention as an explanation for wife beating that it is discussed separately in Chapter 5. The test results for the other four propositions are presented next.

SOCIAL SUPPORT AND ISOLATION

The concepts of social support and isolation can be used in a variety of ways when trying to explain the structural causes of family violence. Social isolation can mean the loneliness and frustration a mother feels at having to raise her children alone, without the help of their father, while support can mean the physical and emotional relief she gets from having her husband actively involved as a caretaker. Or isolation can mean life in nuclear families, separated both physically and emotionally from other families, while support can mean life in an extended family in which grandparents routinely help care for their grandchildren. Support can also mean the understanding women receive from other women in their work group, while isolation can mean the loneliness they feel working alone in their homes. Underlying these and other conceptualizations of social isolation and support is the notion, so pervasive in the family violence literature, that it is the very isolation caused by the absence of physical, material, or emotional support from other individuals or groups that is a basic cause of family violence.

Out of this general perspective come four specific hypotheses for testing here:

(1) Family violence will occur more often in societies in which families are isolated from other families.

(2) Family violence will occur more often in societies in which family members are distant and uninvolved with one another.

(3) Family violence will occur more often in societies in which families have loose ties to the community in general.

(4) Family violence will occur more often in societies in which women have few ties to other women and men have strong ties to other men.

The statistical results of tests of these hypotheses are summarized in Table 4.1.

TABLE 4.1

Social Isolation and Family Violence

	wife beating frequency	child punishment	sibling fighting	husband beating	wife beating severity
household type	−.098	.098	.019	.108	.007
divorce frequency	.062	.008	−.175	.022	.272
postmarital residence	.099	−.193	−.139	.077	−.097
husband-wife sleeping	.151	.061	.062	−.039	−.027
endogamy/exogamy	−.045	−.083	.084	−.067	−.065
female work groups	.304*	−.052	.085	.361*	.216
men's houses	.071	.048	.133	.125	−.087

*Significant at .05 level.

The Isolated Family

A number of researchers and reviewers suggest that, at least in the United States, it is the nuclear family, functioning as an independent social unit isolated from other like families, that creates the conditions for family violence to occur (Gelles, 1974; Keller and Erne, 1983; Levine, 1986; Stark et al., 1981; Straus et al., 1980; Whitehurst, 1974). Among the characteristics of nuclear families that are seen as contributing to a high rate of violence are the amount of time family members spend together, the intensity of their involvement with one another, the number of activities they are involved in, isolation from outside help, and a high level of stress (Gelles and Straus, 1979). While it is easy to trace family violence to the nuclear family, it is not so easy to test the idea with data from only one society in which a single family type predominates. What is needed is a test that allows us to compare violence rates for different types of families. Though this is not possible with the data used here, I can compare our 90 societies in terms of the type of family household that is most common in each: extended, polygynous, nuclear, or mixed (some combination of two or more of these types).

As shown in Table 4.1, household type is not a predictor of any form of violence considered here. This is a surprising finding for two reasons. First, it runs counter to the widely held belief that wife beating will be less common and less severe in extended-family households in which relatives are present to intervene in wife-beating incidents. Second, it fails to support previous cross-cultural research findings that show that child punishment tends to occur more frequently in societies with independent or single-parent households (Munroe and Munroe, 1980; Rohner, 1975, 1986).

As for surprise number one, I think the problem here is a mis-understanding of what life is often like in extended families. Rather than being free and easy with little stress and much mutual support, extended-family life can be quite stressful. As Pasternak et al. (1976: 14) note:

> In addition to the ordinary problems of living in a one-family household, the members of an extended family household might be faced with conflicts of authority between senior and junior individuals or between siblings, conflicts of loyalty because of competing interests of spouses and kinsmen, and other conflicts which may arise merely from the larger number of possible dyads, triads, and so forth.

Surprise number two—the lack of an association between household type and child punishment—is more troubling because it runs counter to findings reported elsewhere. To further test the possibility of an association, I have computed the mean scores on the use of physical punishment for each of the household types. When analyzed this way, the pattern does support the household type—child punishment prediction. Extended-family households have the lowest mean score (2.075), followed by nuclear households (2.10), then mother-child households (2.86), with punishment ranked on a 1-4 scale.

Children in extended-family households are less likely to suffer physical punishment primarily because there are more people available to meet each child's needs and relieve other caretakers from the stress associated with continual child care responsibility (Minturn and Lambert, 1964; Levinson, 1979; Rohner, 1986; Whiting, 1960). The presence of multiple caretakers in the home almost guarantees that an infant or child will have his or her physical and emotional needs met and met more quickly than when only one caretaker is available. However, the relationship of the caretaker to the child does make a difference. Siblings, in general, are not especially warm and loving, but the father or grandparents in the home on a daily basis helps ensure that infants and children will be held and treated warmly. On the other hand, an infant or child is more likely to be emotionally rejected and physically abused when being raised by his or her mother alone. Munroe and Munroe (1980) suggest that multiple family living arrangements might reduce stress associated with child rearing by cutting the time parents are involved in child-rearing activities, curbing parent's emotional outbursts, providing adult targets for blowing off steam, providing adult companionship, and by promoting more cooperative work relationships. The benefits of the availability of multiple caretakers for both the caretakers and the children is made clear by the following example from the Santal of India (Skrefsrud, 1942: 88):

Old men and their wives love their grandchildren very much: they carry them on their hips, they fondle them, and the wives of the brothers also, if they live in peace with each other, carry the children of them all on their hips and fondle them, and when they have fever or are ill, they also nurse each other.

The Uninvolved Family

The issue here is one of family disorganization. When social relations within the family are weak or disorganized we would expect that one manifestation of that disorganization might be violence directed at other family members. Martin and Walter (1982), working with 489 cases in the United States, find, for example, that physical abuse of children is linked to the frequency of parent-child conflicts and Keller and Erne (1983) list a number of other studies also linking child abuse to family disorganization. Cross-cultural research suggests the same conclusion, with Whiting and Whiting (1976) reporting that children who grow up in households in which their parents do not sleep together (suggesting a lack of parental intimacy and warmth) tend to be more aggressive and less warm themselves. Thus there is some reason to consider family disorganization a likely contributor to family violence.

I use four measures of distance and disorganization. Divorce frequency is meant to tap the degree of disorganization, on the assumption that in societies in which divorce occurs in a majority of marriages, family relationships are more likely to be uncertain and unpredictable. The presence of men's houses and husband-wife sleeping arrangements are used to measure the degree of involvement between the husband and wife and father and children. In societies with men's houses (buildings or places where men regularly eat, congregate, and sleep and from which women are excluded) and those in which husbands sleep apart from their wives in a separate room or dwelling, we would expect to find more distance and more violence. Our fourth measure is the type of postmarital residence used in the society, on the assumption that family violence might occur more often in societies in which the wife must live with her husband's family.

As shown in Table 4.1, these factors are, at best, weak predictors of family violence. Further examination of postmarital residence patterns suggests that which family the couple lives with and whether they live alone or with one or the other's family are unrelated to any form of family violence. Thus there seems little support for the proposition that family violence is more likely to occur in families with distant and disorganized social relations.

The Disassociated Family

In the first two hypotheses I was interested in the ties families have to other families, family units, or individuals within the family. Here I am interested in the degree to which the family is embedded in its community. Resource, exchange, and ecological theory all predict that families with strong ties to the community would experience less family violence than would those with weak ties. I use two measures of community ties: First, the type of marriage—endogamy—in which the husband and wife both come from the same community, versus exogamy—in which they come from different communities. Second, type of postmarital residence with residence patterns in which the couple has a choice (neolocal or mixed) compared to those in which there is no choice (patrilocal or matrilocal). We would expect to find family violence tied to exogamous marriage and to a choice in postmarital residence, as both suggest distance from the community either for both or one partner. The correlations for endogamy-exogamy in Table 4.1 run opposite to the prediction for four of the five family violence types, although all the coefficients are weak. And the correlations for postmarital residence fail to support the hypothesis as well. Thus we can conclude that the degree of family involvement in the community is not a predictor of family violence. However, it is worth keeping in mind that community involvement might indirectly affect family violence by influencing the nature and level of a community's response to family violence incidents, a point discussed further in Chapter 7, where I take up more complex explanations for the absence of family violence.

The Isolated Wife

Studies in the United States suggest a wife's involvement in the community (number of communities activities, contact with friends, and so on) is not necessarily a predictor of wife beating (Bowker, 1983; Hotaling and Sugarman, 1986). However, as discussed In Chapter 5, there is some evidence that women who stay at home and do not work are at somewhat greater risk than are women who do work. This is probably because women who stay at home contribute less to family subsistence and are consequently valued less than women who work outside the home. In any wife-beating incident there is always a risk to the husband that he will anger his wife to the point that she leaves him. This is more costly to men whose wives contribute directly to subsistence.

Following this line of reasoning, I examine here the effect on family violence of women's participation in exclusively female work groups. Exclusively female work groups exist in 22% of the societies in our sample and range from women regularly working side-by-side in the fields, to female traders who go to market together each week, to women's economic associations. In rural Okinawa, for example, married women under 57 years of age join the village women's associations that exist to modernize women's lives by easing "the burdens of daily life and presence of poverty" (Maretzki and Maretzki 1963: 418). In rural Greece, women's work groups take the form of the *nychteria*, groups of women who gather together in the evening to complete household chores and to talk, sing, dance, and joke (Sanders, 1962). And at a somewhat less organized level are societies such as the Bushmen of South Africa in which women regularly work side-by-side gathering food (Marshall, 1965).

Table 4.1 indicates that the absence of such groups is a predictor of the frequency and a weaker predictor of the severity of wife beating. This finding provides considerable support for the resource and exchange theories of wife beating. Evidently, wife beating will be far less common in societies in which women have independent economic and social resources, perhaps because those resources are valuable enough to make a husband think twice before acting in ways that might force his wife to terminate the marriage.

Because of the strong relationship to frequency, it is useful to examine this pattern in more detail. Analysis shows that it is not so much the absence of work groups that predicts frequent wife beating but the presence of such groups that predicts infrequent wife beating. Of the 20 societies with exclusively female work groups 80% have no or infrequent wife beating, as compared to 53% for the entire 90-society sample. Thus it appears that the presence of exclusively female work groups, whether an indicator of female solidarity or of female economic power, or both, serves to control or prevent wife beating.

Related to the question of the wife's involvement in the community is the question of the husband's. This issue has already been discussed in Chapter 3 and is discussed indirectly next.

The Macho Male

"Compulsive masculinity," "defensive masculinity," "protest masculinity," "hyperaggressive masculinity," and "compensatory machoism" are all names for what in polite social science circles is called the male sex identity conflict. Beatrice Whiting (1965: 126-27) provides the clearest statement of the sex identity conflict hypothesis:

> In simplest terms, the theory states that an individual identifies with that person who seems most important to him, the person who is perceived as controlling those resources that he wants. If during the first two or three years of life a child is constantly with his mother and infrequently sees, and is handled by, his father, he will identify strongly with his mother and not with his father; in short, if he is a boy he will have a cross-sex identification. If, later in life, he is involved in a world that is obviously dominated by men, a world in which men are perceived to be more prestigeful and powerful than women, he will be thrown into conflict. He will develop a strong need to reject his underlying female identity. This may lead to an overdetermined attempt to prove his masculinity, manifested by a preoccupation with physical strength and athletic prowess, or attempts to demonstrate daring and valor, or behavior that is violent and aggressive. These types of behavior will be referred to as "protest masculinity."

There is considerable cross-cultural evidence that a male sex identity conflict as measured by polygynous marriage (wives and their children usually sleep apart from the father), a long postpartum sex taboo, exclusive mother-child sleeping arrangements, or father absence from the home is associated with a variety of violent and aggressive behaviors. These include bride theft, warlikeness, glorification of violence, assault, homicide, drunken brawling, and feuding (Ayres, 1974; Bacon et al., 1963; Howe, 1966; Minturn and Lambert, 1964; Straus, 1977; Whiting, 1969; Whiting and D'Andrade, 1959). However, the cross-cultural record also suggests that violence is not the only way the conflict can be resolved. Initiation ceremonies for boys involving genital operations (circumcision or subincision) and the couvade are two institutionalized means that help resolve the conflict (Munroe et al., 1981). Initiation ceremonies of this type occur most commonly in societies with patrilocal residence and serve to turn feminine boys into masculine men. The view that initiation ceremonies serve as an alternative to hyperaggressive behavior in adulthood is supported by the finding reported in Chapter 3, that initiation ceremonies are unrelated to the frequency of either wife beating or child punishment. The couvade provides a ritualized means for men to express their female identity in matrilocal societies in which women are more likely than they are in patrilocal societies to have power and prestige equal to that of men. By adopting the symptoms of and behaving like their pregnant wives, men are able to express their feminine identity without jeopardizing their public identity as males.

While the cross-cultural evidence points to a clear and consistent relationship between an unresolved male sex identity conflict and violent behavior, Rosenbaum (1986) suggests that the case may be overstated for the United States. His own psychometric data comparing groups of violent, unhappy nonviolent, and happy nonviolent husbands suggests that sex identity is not directly linked to wife beating. As an alternative explanation he suggests, following Carter et al. (1984), that when men are without a clear sex role identity, they act in ways that they believe men should act, which may involve violence in the home if that was part of their own upbringing. Male sex identity conflicts are so common because they are the indirect result of two structural features characteristic of nearly all societies around the world. First, in nearly all societies the division of labor by sex places the primary responsibility for child rearing on women. Thus it is almost inevitable that all children, whether boys or girls, will spend much time with their mothers. Second, in nearly all societies men are expected to act like men (in accord with the cultural definition of maleness) and women are expected to act like women (in accord with the cultural definition of femaleness). Thus, putting these two factors together with a third—that in many societies men's work is outside the home—it is not surprising that male sex identity conflicts occur nearly everywhere.

Our primary interest here is the relationship between the male sex identity conflict and family violence, particularly wife beating. I indirectly measure the presence of an identity conflict in two ways: the presence/absence of men's houses and husband-wife sleeping arrangements. Each measure taps to some extent the role of the father in child rearing and the degree of contact the children are likely to have with their mother. Using a more direct measure such as the actual involvement of the father in child rearing is not feasible because most ethnographers report that the mother plays the primary role in infant and child care and report little about the father's role. As noted previously, men's houses are buildings or places where single and married men congregate, often sleep, and from which women are excluded. The presence of men's houses suggests that men are often absent from the household and uninvolved in child rearing. Husband-wife sleeping arrangements also measure father involvement on a scale ranging from "husband-wife share the same bed," to "they share the same dwelling but not the same bed," to "the husband occasionally sleeps elsewhere," to "the husband and wife occupy separate dwellings." The rho coefficient of .39* between these two variables suggests that they are measuring the same phenomenon.

Table 4.2 shows weak relationships between men's houses and sleeping arrangements and violence. I have included drunken brawling and warfare ethos as indicators of the possible effect of the sex identity conflict on aggression outside the family. Evidently, a sex identity

TABLE 4.2
The Macho Male Hypothesis

	Men's Houses	Husband-Wife Sleeping
wife beating	.071	.151
child punishment	.048	.061
drunken brawling	.158	−.026
warfare ethos	.100	.114

conflict does not necessarily lead to violent behavior. But, this finding does not preclude the possibility that a sex identity conflict in combination with other factors such as the violent resolution of adult conflicts or male dominance does lead to more family violence.

SOCIAL COMPLEXITY AND FAMILY VIOLENCE

The notion that family violence will occur more frequently in societies with more complex social, economic, and political systems is the broadest of the four structural approaches examined here. This proposition, of course, reflects the cultural evolution perspective that suggests that different levels of cultural complexity require the development of different social structures, values, and behaviors. As the broadest approach, the complexity hypothesis is of considerable theoretical but of limited practical importance since any violence prevention program based on the complexity model would, by definition, require a basic restructuring of society.

As generally used in the social sciences, social complexity refers to the relative degree of differentiation and specialization in a society. Differentiation refers to the separating-out of elements of the cultural system from one another. In simple societies the kinship, economic, and political subsystems are often so intertwined that it is difficult to tell where one begins and the other ends. But, in more complex societies, the boundaries between the subsystems are often much clearer. Specialization refers to the elaboration of elements of the cultural system. More complex specialization means that a society has a larger inventory of cultural traits and a greater variety of trait types. Dozens of cross-cultural studies provide us with a lengthy list of the differences between simple and complex societies (for reviews, see Berreman, 1978 and Levinson and Malone, 1980). Simple societies tend to have small, isolated, homogeneous populations, close social relations, generalized roles, limited control over their environment, communal ownership of valuable property, informal social control mechanisms, and wealth sharing. Complex societies, on the other hand, tend to have large, dense, heterogeneous populations, distant social relations, specialized roles, strong control over their environment, private ownership of property, formal social control mechanisms, and wealth hoarding.

The Yanoama of southern Venezuela and northern Brazil and the Serbs of Yugoslavia are examples of societies near the low and high ends of the scale of cultural complexity. The Yanoama are a group of Indian tribes numbering about 12,000 people who live in about 200 villages in the tropical rain forest. They subsist primarily on the plantains, bananas, and other tropical crops they grow by means of slash and burn horticulture, supplemented by animals they hunt and wild plant foods they gather. The villages are lightly populated and ruled by a headman who achieves his status by either inheriting the position or earning the support of relatives in the village. The Serbs are a group of over eight million people who live on farms, in villages, and in cities in the Republic of Serbia in Yugoslavia. They subsist by growing their own wheat and corn and raising livestock, growing barley and oats for trade at the market, and wage labor. Each village is governed by an elected council with the Yugoslav government providing a variety of services.

Not only do these two societies serve as examples of simple and complex societies, they also demonstrate the relationship between social complexity and family violence that seems to exist around the world. Our research supports the conclusion, reported elsewhere (Petersen et al., 1982; Pryor, 1977; Rohner, 1986), that physical punishment of children is more likely to occur in complex societies. Child punishment is related both to a larger population (rho = .27*) and to level of dependence on agriculture (rho = .42*). Among the Yanoama, child punishment is virtually absent with parent's preferring "gentle admonishment" despite frequent and brutal wife beatings and frequent ritualized chest-pounding duels and club fights between men (Becher, 1960). Among the Serbs, physical punishment is commonplace, used regularly in 95% of the 300 households surveyed by Erlich (1965). Not surprisingly, I also find sibling aggression linked to population (rho = .21), evidently, as I suggested in Chapter 2, because older siblings model their caretaking behavior on that of their parents. On the other hand, neither wife-beating frequency or severity (rho = .03, –.14) nor husband beating (rho = –.14) is associated with complexity as measured by the size of the population.

Why physical punishment is used more often by parents in complex societies than by parents in simpler societies it not clear, although

Petersen and his colleagues (1982) suggest a plausible explanation. They reason that in complex societies adults are more likely to be supervised by others. Therefore, adults value conformity and use physical punishment to inculcate conformity in their children. Peterson et al.'s path analysis supports this interpretation, with a value on conformity and physical punishment associated with an economy requiring complex work teams, a political hierarchy, kin ties to both the husband's and wife's family, and a belief that ancestors influence the affairs of the living.

SOCIAL CHANGE

It is generally assumed that in non-Western societies industrialization, modernization, Westernization, and the like create social disorganization that leads, in turn, to an increase in social problems, such as crime, delinquency, substance abuse, and family violence. Social change is seen as altering traditional family structures, dynamics, and values that places new and additional stress on individuals and the family and destroys the social support network in which the family was embedded. Of course, this line of reasoning rests on the assumption that family violence tends to be absent in non-Western societies, an assumption I have questioned in Chapter 2. However, from the limited data at hand, it appears that social change can increase the frequency of family violence, decrease the frequency, produce changes in how violence is defined, or lead to new forms of family violence. Korbin (1981), for example, points out that following contact with Western culture, behaviors that are defined as child abuse by Western standards tend to disappear, but new practices appear, such as having children sleep alone or leaving them in the care of nonrelatives that are considered abusive in the traditional context.

Societies for which I have evidence that these types of changes have occurred are listed in Table 4.3. Of course, this listing is not based on a systematic survey, but on what reports are currently available in the literature. Still, the distribution of the cases does give a sense that the effect of social change is not as predictable as one might assume.

One of the more interesting patterns I found is the direct effect that social change can have on increasing the frequency of wife beating. In two of the societies in which wife beating increased, ethnographers report that it was the direct result of outsiders deliberately changing traditional marriage practices. The first of the societies is the reservation

TABLE 4.3
Social Change and Family Violence

Increase in Family Violence		
Hare of Canada	wife beating	(Savishinsky, 1970)
Bororo of Brazil	wife beating	(Baldus, 1937)
Ojibwa of Wisconsin	wife beating	(Landes, 1937)
Mossi of Mali	wife beating	(Hammond, 1964)
Serbs of Yugoslavia	wife beating	(Erlich, 1966)
Kpelle of Liberia	wife beating	(Erchak, 1984)
Sub-Saharan Africa	child neglect	(LeVine and LeVine, 1981)
Decrease in Family Violence		
Greece (rural)	wife beating	(Sanders, 1962)
Azande of Central Africa	wife beating	(Evans-Pritchard, 1937)
Ganda of Uganda	wife beating	(Mair, 1940)
Somali of Somalia	wife beating	(Lewis, 1962)
Quechua of Ecuador	wife beating	(Muratoria, 1981)
New Types of Family Violence		
Sri Lanka	child labor	(deSilva, 1981)
Zulu of South Africa	child neglect	(Loening, 1981)
Nigeria	patricide and matricide	(Nkpa, 1981)
Japan	filial violence	(Kumagai, 1981)
Tahiti	youth violence	(Spiegal, 1981)

Ojibwa, where U.S. government agents routinely forced unhappy couples to remain together:

> James Leonard is always very sulky towards his young wife, and sometimes he stays away for days gambling. At such time his wife, Janet, goes to her mother's home and cries herself to sleep. Janet used to protest to her husband, and "they would throw lip at one another and take to fighting." Several times Janet's mother, Mrs. Wilson, found her in bed helpless from her husband's kicks. . . . But the Agent said they had to live together, otherwise he wouldn't help James with his wheat. I tried to tell the Agent that they should separate, but he said no [Landes, 1937: 83].

Such action is not restricted to American Indian reservations or to government officials. Among the Bororo of Brazil, it was the missionaries, in their zeal to prevent divorce, who indirectly encouraged wife beating: "In the past they would separate when the marriage was not going well; today, however, the marriages being Christian, and thus indissoluble, the husband would thrash the woman"(Baldus, 1937: 148). These examples are not meant to imply that all changes in family violence patterns are the result of the actions of outsiders. But they do serve to remind us that the everyday impact of Westernization, modernization, and other such powerful processes are often realized through the actions taken by outsiders in close contact with the indigenous society.

Perhaps the most important conclusion I can make about social change and family violence from the data available here is that the short-and long-term effects of social change might be quite different. Two examples make this point. The first case is the Hare Indians of Colville Lake in Canada's Northwest Territories (Savishinsky, 1976). About 60 Hare and 10 whites live in the village, although the Hare occupy their cabins only about six months a year, spending the other six months in the "bush," hunting, fishing and trapping. Contact with the outside world is mainly through trips to Fort Good Hope, a town of about 325 people 110 miles to the south that offers a school, a nurse, a store, a government office, and an air strip. In the 1960s life in Colville Lake began to change as the younger people started to adopt "white" ways while the older Hare clung to their traditional culture. These acculturated young people began to speak English as well as their native language. They attended school. They spent more time in Fort Good Hope, and opted for Western leisure activities, such as card playing, sports, and listening to the radio. They also suffered from "cultural disorientation" characterized by a breakdown of their personality structure owing to the erosion of their traditional ways and beliefs in the absence of any suitable replacements.

One sign of cultural disorientation was the appearance of wife beating (Savishinsky, 1976: 210-211):

> Such wife beating and disruptive behavior occur only among the most acculturated and disoriented people, the less acculturated drinkers being much quieter and basically nonviolent. Wife beating often occurs outside the house and in full view of other villagers. People call out, "free show" and come out to watch. As long as no one is getting badly hurt, they talk, laugh, comment, but will eventually intervene if someone is getting hurt.

The second example is the peasant peoples of the Macedonia, Bosnia, Serbia, Croatia, and Littoral regions of Yugoslavia (Erlich, 1966). Until the turn of the century in most regions, and until later in others, the Yugoslavian peasants lived in large, extended-family households called *zadrugas*. Each *zadruga* had about 40 members and was ruled by the oldest man, although his sons shared in decision making and his wife had control over the other women. Sons spent their entire lives in the *zadruga* of their birth, with their wives marrying in and their sisters marrying out.

A shift to a money economy beginning around 1900, political disruptions caused by World War I, and the economic depression of the 1930s led to a gradual break-up of the *zadrugas*, first into smaller extended families and then into nuclear families. In the traditional *zadruga*, men held all authority, women "knew their place" and were never beaten. In the years during the transition from the *zadruga* to the smaller extended household, women's status increased, men's decreased, and wife beating became common. Finally, when households stabilized as either small extended or nuclear ones, wife beating virtually disappeared and women's status now equalled that of men. In the Littoral region, which is furthest along this transition to the nuclear family household, wife beating is nonexistent and women contribute equally to decision making in 85% of the villages surveyed.

These two examples provide three lessons for future research on the relationship between social change and family violence. First, it is best to view social change as an open-ended, long-term process rather than as a narrow cause and effect sequence. Second, social change involves both internal and external forces. Third, social change can lead to both more and less family violence; it is not "change" that's necessarily important, but the kind and consequences of change.

SUMMARY

In this chapter, I have examined a variety of social structural features of society in terms of their relationship to family violence. My central conclusion is that structural features alone do not cause family violence. However, certain structural forces do effect family violence. Children in extended-family households are less likely to be physically punished than are children in single-parent or nuclear family households. When wives are members of exclusively female economic groups, they are unlikely to be beaten by their husbands. Children in societies with more complex socioeconomic systems are more likely to be physically punished, perhaps because their parents are especially concerned with obedience and compliance. And, social change may lead to less, more, or new forms of family violence. I can now turn to another and, perhaps the most important structural factor—sexual inequality.

-5-

WIFE BEATING AND SEXUAL INEQUALITY

Of all the different explanations for wife beating none has drawn so much attention as the so-called sexual inequality theory. Depending on how broadly sexual inequality is defined, the concept of sexual inequality enters into resource, exchange, social learning, patriarchal, and general systems perspectives on family violence. I suspect that it has garnered so much support because of its simplicity and its commonsense appeal. It makes sense to assume that husbands will beat their wives when men have more power and status than women have, and can use that superiority to control the behavior of their wives. Thus if the sexual inequality theory is correct, wife beating can be viewed as one means men use to control women, and at the same time, the presence of wife beating can be taken as evidence that men do, in fact, control women in a family or society.

Sexual inequality theory can be conceptualized and tested at both the family and societal level. At the family level, the theory predicts that wife beating will be more frequent in families in which the husband has more power and status than the wife has. At the societal level, the theory predicts that wife beating will be more frequent in societies in which men have more power and prestige than women have.

Although most tests of sexual inequality theory have focused on the family, advocates of patriarchal theory stress the societal roots of sexual inequality. Del Martin (1983: 26), in her influential, *Battered Wives*, summarizes the basics of the argument:

> The historical roots of our patriarchal family models are ancient and deep. The task of tearing them up and establishing more equitable human relations is a formidable one. Still, new norms for marriage and family must be created, since the battering of wives grows naturally out of ancient, time-honored traditions.

Dobash and Dobash (1979: 33-34) review the record of Western civilization and reach the same conclusion:

> The seeds of wife beating lie in the subordination of females and in their subjection to male authority and control. The relationship between women and men has been institutionalized in the structure of the

patriarchal family and is supported by the economic and political institutions and by a belief system, including a religious one, that makes such relationships seem natural, morally just and sacred. This structure and ideology can be seen most starkly in the records of two societies that provided the roots of our cultural legacy, the Romans and the early Christians.

As suggested by the descriptive information on wife beating summarized in Chapter 2, wife beating incidents are often linked with male dominance and control in many societies around the world. As you may recall, in our analysis of types of wife beating, three types of male control were identified: (1) control of women's sexuality as evidenced by wife beating for adultery; (2) control of women's behavior as evidenced by wife beating for lack of or poor performance of female duties; and (3) control of women's lives as evidenced by beatings at will. The purpose of this chapter is to go beyond these descriptive findings and report the results of tests of sexual inequality theory at the societal level.

Despite the broad interest in sexual inequality theory, only two cross-cultural comparative studies have addressed the question empirically. Unfortunately, they provide contradictory conclusions. Masamura (1979) argues that sexual inequality is unrelated to wife beating as his analysis of data for 86 societies shows no relationship between wife beating and either patrilocal postmarital residence or patrilineal descent. This finding is not surprising, as I too (see Table 5.1) find only a weak association between postmarital residence and wife beating. However, as discussed next, a focus on only these two factors provides only a partial test of sexual inequality theory. Lester's (1980) analysis of data for 71 societies shows a relationship between inequality and wife beating, although he provides no indication of how inequality is measured, a crucial issue in any test of sexual inequality theory.

WHAT IS SEXUAL INEQUALITY?

Most of us can easily recognize signs of inequality between women and men in American society. Women are paid less than men are for work that requires equal skill and effort. Women more often hold jobs that offer less opportunity for advancement. Working women perform more household chores than their working husbands do. Wives are expected to take their husband's surname upon marriage. Divorce often raises a man's economic well-being while lowering a woman's, and so forth. Thus it is easy to pick out signs of sexual inequality in our own society. But, how do we define and measure sexual inequality in a sample of 90 different societies? The basic rules and procedures are set forth in Martin Whyte's (1978a: 107-108), *The Status of Women in Preindustrial Society.*

Whyte collected and analyzed data on 52 indicators of female status for a worldwide sample of 98 societies and concluded:

> While small groups of discrete measures of aspects of the status of women can be formed into coherent scales, and while a few of these have consistent patterns of association with some others, the thrust of our results is that there is a large amount of independent variation in aspects of what we have been considering the general status of women.... Clearly we are dealing with very complex phenomena.

Whyte goes on to suggest that female status is composed of at least nine separate dimensions: property control, kinship power, value of women's lives, value of women's labor, domestic authority, separation of the sexes, control of marriage and sex, fear of women, and male-female joint participation. The lesson from Whyte's work and the principle that guides my work is that different aspects of female status may be differentially related to wife-beating frequency. Thus, rather than testing sexual inequality theory in its general form, I have tested specific predictions derived from the general theory.

Before discussing my conceptualization of sexual inequality, it seems useful to show how a woman's status can vary in a society. Consider the Dogon, an agricultural society of some 250,000 people in Mali, West Africa. Denise Paulme (1940: 260), a leading expert on Dogon social organization, describes female status succinctly: "The man is master in the street, but inside the house the woman recovers her rights and has her own way." However, variations in status among Dogon women go further and deeper than public images and private realities. In some ways, Dogon wives are the equal of their husbands. They can amass individual wealth, inherit property on nearly equal terms as men, divorce their husbands as easily as their husbands can divorce them, and engage just as freely in premarital sexual relations. But, in a number of ways, men have the advantage. Men, but not women, work in sex-segregated work groups, husbands own the family dwelling, men can take more than one wife, a husband's relatives pick the new husband for his widow, and menstruating women are considered unclean and their activities restricted. The Dogon are a good example of the lack of patterning of female status characteristic of many societies around the world. Just as Whyte found in 1978, status in one sphere of activity is often unrelated to the degree of status afforded women in other spheres.

Another aspect of inequality that requires comment is the public versus private status and power of women. Although the data do not enable us to systematically consider this manifestation of inequality, it should be noted that in some societies status acknowledged within the household is distinct from public status. There are at least two variations of this pattern: First, are societies in which men and women have complementary power, with women having authority over female activities and other women in the household, and men having authority over male activities and other males. The Serbs of Yugoslavia and Saraksanti of Greece are two societies with this pattern, although in both cases the husband does have ultimate authority in the household. This complementary pattern seems confined mainly to societies with large, extended households in which the wife/mother can supervise the work of her sons' wives.

The second variation of this pattern is found in societies in which wives have authority in the domestic sphere and sometimes in the economic sphere as well, but public acknowledgment of that authority is not permitted. This pattern is suggested by the status of Dogon women described here, with a more dramatic example provided by the Igbo of Nigeria. Although Igbo men are generally dominant over Igbo women, wives do have some degree of authority in the household and are able to spend as they see fit the proceeds from the sale of cassava that they grow and sell. However, the public image must always be that of male dominance (Anyasodo, 1975: 89):

> One day, Ike suddenly invites some of his male friends for a dinner without any adequate notice to Ada. But like an understanding wife, who wants to please her husband, she manages to use a greater amount of the small money left to purchase things for the visitors' dinner.

> As the last visitor leaves, Ike furiously demands to know from Ada why she has not bought enough wine for their visitors. Ada's passive silence and aloofness make Ike so angry that he slaps her.

> Unexpectedly, Ada seizes him by the collar, throws him on the floor, sits on top of Ike, and with two hands starts pounding him like the pistons of a steam locomotive in full speed. The pounding, kicking and shouting attract the attention of the villagers and send some of them running to investigate.

> As the sounds of the running footsteps grow louder, Ada in a quick maneuver throws herself on the floor, lifts Ike up to her stomach and starts screaming. Ike, who is now sitting on Ada's stomach, starts throwing some powerless punches at her.

> The villagers are startled as they rush in to see Ike with the bruised face and bleeding nose. Ada, while still lying on the floor, keeps screaming for help without throwing any punches back at her husband.

While this a fairly dramatic example, it does show a pattern that in other societies is manifested in women walking behind their husbands, or women keeping quiet in public, or never openly questioning their husband's judgement.

Reflecting the belief that sexual inequality as measured by differences in status and power is a multidimensional phenomenon, I have chosen to define and measure sexual inequality as the difference between men and women in status, power or prestige in six spheres of human activity: control of wealth and property, dominance in the household, restrictions on sex and marriage, separation of the sexes, value of human life, and structuring of kinship relations. The specific variables for these six spheres are listed in Table 5.1 with details on measures and coding supplied in Appendix B.

HYPOTHESES TESTED

Six specific hypotheses linking sexual inequality to wife beating are tested. Not only does this more focused hypothesis-testing approach aid in identifying causes of wife beating but it also provides more useful information relevant to the control and prevention of wife beating. The six hypotheses suggest that wife beating will be associated with (1) male dominance in the control of property and wealth, (2) male dominance in the household, (3) restrictions on female sexual and marital freedom, (4) ritualized separation of the sexes, (5) low value placed on female lives, and (6) male dominance in the structuring of kinship relationships.

TEST RESULTS

As shown in Table 5.1, none of the six hypotheses is supported entirely. The correlation coefficients in the table indicate that wife beating is likely to occur more frequently in societies in which men control the fruits of family labor, men have the final say in domestic decision making, divorce is more difficult for women than for men, women do not band together in exclusively female work groups, the husband's kin group controls his widow's right to remarry, and polygynous marriage is permitted (although I find no evidence that wife beating is more common in polygynous than in monogamous marriages). The findings in the table also indicate that some presumed

TABLE 5.1
Sexual Inequality and Wife Beating

Property/wealth control	
inheritance of valuable property	.121
ownership of dwelling	.221
control of fruits of family labor	.252*
independent female wealth	.214
Kin-context power	
type of marriage	.243*
postmarital residence	.099
Value of life of women	
infanticide sex preference	.151
Domestic authority	
domestic decision making	.454*
responsibility for care of boys over 5 years of age	−.016
responsibility for socialization for boys between 5 and 10	
years of age	.032
principal disciplinarian	.228
Ritualized separation of the sexes	
female work groups	.304*
menstrual taboo elaboration	.180
female initiation rites	.049
Control over sex and marriage	
premarital double standard	.055
widow remarriage freedom	.274*
divorce freedom	.239*

*Significant at .05 level.

predictors of wife beating such as female inheritance rights, female infanticide, elaborate menstrual taboos, and patrilocal postmarital residence probably have little to do with the frequency of wife beating in societies around the world. Thus these 17 coefficients in Table 5.1 suggest that sexual inequality is associated with wife beating, although the relationship may be more complex than a simple one-to-one association between specific aspects of inequality and wife beating.

AN ECONOMIC INEQUALITY MODEL

A more complex explanation for the inequality-wife beating relationship is provided in Figure 5.1. This economic model, developed from the results reported in Table 5.1 and intercorrelations among the sexual inequality measures suggests that male control of wealth and property is the basic cause of wife beating. However, the model also suggests that the influence of male economic control is mediated by the degree of male authority in the household and by the severity of divorce restrictions placed on women. Thus wife beating is likely to be frequent in a society when men control the wealth, have the final say in household decision making, and are able to prevent their wives from escaping from the marriage through divorce.

Economic control includes four factors, all of which are inter-correlated (rhos range from .19 to .37). Control of fruits of labor refers to control over the distribution of monetary or material products of the labor of household members. Inheritance refers to a preference for male or females or neither in the passing on of economically valuable property or wealth. Control of female wealth refers to whether or not women are allowed to amass and control wealth, by having an independent income, by retaining control of wealth they bring to the marriage, or by being free to use a portion of the family wealth for their own needs. The fourth economic control factor, dwelling ownership, indicates whether the husband or his family, the wife or her family, or both own the family dwelling.

Domestic authority, one of the two intervening variables, and the single most powerful predictor of wife-beating frequency, refers to inequality in making decisions involving the use of family resources, the children, the family life-style, and so on. Divorce freedom refers to the severity of restrictions placed on wives relative to those placed on husbands.

Support for this economic model comes from three sources, although it is important to note that, since the model was developed post hoc, it requires further cross-cultural testing with a new sample of societies before it can be thought of as having been tested cross-culturally. The first source of support is the rho coefficients reported in Figure 5.1. These coefficients indicate that the four economic factors are more consistently related to the two intervening factors (domestic authority and divorce freedom) than they are to wife-beating frequency. These coefficients also demonstrate that domestic authority, divorce freedom, and control of fruits of family labor are the most powerful predictors of wife beating of the six causal factors in the model, with only female work groups (rho = .30*), to be discussed next, an equally powerful predictor.

The second source of support for the model comes from a partial correlational analysis, focusing on the relationship between the economic factors and wife-beating frequency when the effects of domestic

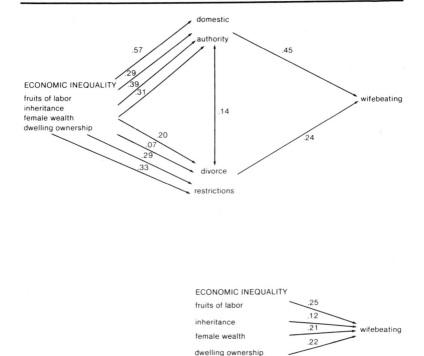

Figure 5.1. Economic Inequality Model.

authority and divorce restrictions are controlled. In all cases, the correlations are weaker when the effects of the intervening variables are controlled. Thus it is clear that the influence of male economic control on wife beating is mediated by male domestic authority and divorce restrictions placed on women.

The third source of support comes from studies of wife beating and sexual inequality in the United States. These studies, of course, bear only indirectly on the cross-cultural model presented here, as they use data derived from only one society and focus primarily on wife beating, economic inequality, and domestic authority at the family rather than the societal level. Kalmuss and Straus (1984) report that a wife's economic dependence on her husband is a major predictor of severe wife beating. Economic dependence is reflected in the wife being unemployed, the presence of children under the age of five in the home, and the husband earning more than 75% of the family income. Yllö (1983; 1984) reports the results of two studies using U.S. states rather than families as the sampling units. In the 1983 study (an analysis of women's legal, political, economic, and educational status and wife beating frequency), Yllö reports a curvilinear relationship between status and wife beating. Wife beating occurs most frequently in those states where women's status is lowest, least frequently in states where women's status is at a mid-range, and with a midlevel of frequency in states where women's status is highest. In Kalmuss and Straus's 1984 study, this finding was retested with the Straus et al. (1980) national survey data based on 2,143 couples. The findings are consistent with Yllö's 1983 study: in U.S. states the relationship between wife beating and female status is curvilinear. Yllö and others suggest that this pattern may reflect a transitional state in which family norms and societal norms governing expectations about status distinctions are incongruent. This transition and incongruence leads some men to try and reinforce their decreasing authority in the home by beating their wives. This interpretation is supported by Erlich's (1966) study of social change over a 40-year period in 300 Yugoslav villages. Erlich's findings suggest that a shift from a male-dominant to a egalitarian social order is a multigenerational process, with the frequency of family violence likely to first increase and then decline during the process.

A number of other studies report results relevant to the domestic authority-wife beating linkage. Adler (1981), in a study of graduate school couples, finds that wife beating occurs far more often in marriages in which the husband dominates domestic decision making. Bowker's (1983) study of 146 volunteer couples in Milwaukee provides the same conclusion, with wife beating more common in families in which the husband makes the decisions. Bowker also reports that wife beating tends to decrease in frequency when decision making becomes more egalitarian. In a recent article, Coleman and Straus (1986) use the 2,143-family national survey data and report that both the actual power distribution in the family and shared understandings about what the distribution should be influence the level of violence.

To sum up, consideration of both these findings about American couples and the cross-cultural findings reported here provide support for the economic inequality model as an explanation for wife beating.

Sexual Inequality and Wife Beating Among the Saraktsani

The Saraktsani are a Greek-speaking society of some 100,000 goat and sheep herders who live in the mountains of Northern Greece. The Saraktsani live in large, extended families bound together by a strong sense of family, pride, honor, and strength. Wife beating among the

Saraktsani is "at will," and women believe that "When you are married you are enslaved because God wills it so" (Campbell, 1964: 153).

The Saraktsani are a living example of the sexual-inequality model described in statistical terms here. To a large extent, husbands and wives have complementary roles, with the husband handling external matters and the wife running the day-to-day household (Campbell, 1964). But, the husband clearly has the final say in economic and other matters. He manages the flocks, negotiates family business affairs, protects his wife's honor, and arranges the marriages of his children. Although daughters take a small dowry with them upon marriage, it is the sons who inherit the livestock and other property. Divorce is rare, perhaps because a husband is expected to kill an adulterous wife and her lover, a situation that might lead to divorce in other societies. When divorce does occur, the husband is expected to initiate it. Thus one can reasonably argue that among the Saraktsani and many other societies, economic power provides husbands with ultimate control over the household and their wives' freedom, which, in turn, allows them to beat their wives.

Female Work Groups and Wife Beating

The second strongest predictor of wife-beating frequency across our 90-society sample (see Table 5.1) is the absence of exclusively female work groups. An exclusively female work group is a group composed solely of women who meet on an ongoing and regular basis to carry out some economic activity. Exclusively female work groups are not all that common, and are reported as occurring in only 20 of the 90 societies in our sample. These groups take a variety of forms, including groups of female traders, women's village associations, and sex-segregated work teams. As discussed in Chapter 7, it is the presence of female work groups that predicts infrequent or nonexistent wife beating in a society because such groups provide women with a stable social support network as well as economic independence from their husbands and families.

GENITAL MODIFICATIONS AS A FORM OF FAMILY VIOLENCE

Probably no issue concerning family violence and sexual inequality has produced such heated debate as the modification of the genitals of girls and female adolescents in African and Middle Eastern societies.

Before getting to the specifics of the debate, I will briefly describe these modifications and their distribution around the world (Gregerson, 1982; Hosken, 1982). Modifications of the female genitals come in four major forms: (1) *sunna* circumcision—removal of the clitoral prepuce and the tip of the clitoris; (2) clitoridectomy—removal of the clitoris; (3) excision—removal of some or all of the labia minora and/or majora; and (4) infibulation—sewing up the labia majora leaving only a small opening for urination. These procedures are not necessarily mutually exclusive, with clitoridectomy and excision often performed together. Modifications of the male genitals come in three major forms: (1) circumcision—removal of the foreskin; (2) superincision—slitting of the foreskin lengthwise without removal; and (3) subincision—slitting of the underside of the penis lengthwise down to the urethra.

Genital modification operations are performed mainly on girls or boys, although there is considerable variation from society to society in the exact age at which the operation is performed. In most societies the operation is performed by nonfamily members, although family members are sometimes present and always approve of or encourage the procedure. Female modifications are confined primarily to tribal groups in Africa, with excision/clitoridectomy occurring in a number of groups across Africa along the Equator, and infibulation most common in Somali, Mali, and the southern Middle East. Circumcision, the most common form of genital modification, occurs primarily in Africa and the Middle East and the United States. Superincision is confined to a few Oceanic societies, with subincision found in Australia. The ethnographic record suggests that female modifications occur only in societies in which male modifications also occur, although female operations are almost always more extensive, more painful, and more health-threatening.

Because of the severity of female operations, the ongoing debate over what genital operations mean, what purpose they serve, and whether they should be controlled focuses on female modifications. There are three sides to the debate. On one side are those who view such modifications as a mechanism men use to control the lives of women:

> Genital mutilation can only be understood in the psychological climate created by the all-pervasive male sexual violence that forms the unseen background of African and Middle Eastern family life [Hosken, 1982: 30].

A similar position is taken by Daly (1978). In support of this position, Hosken cites the widespread effects such operations have on the estimated 84 million African women who have undergone them. These effects include death resulting from the operation, lifelong health problems, such as urinary infections and childbirth complications, and the emotional trauma caused by an inability to reach orgasm, painful intercourse, and chronic menstrual pain. This view is supported as well by evidence that clitoridectomies were performed in Europe and the United States in the late nineteenth and early twentieth centuries to control female masturbation and reduce women's sex drive (Frayser, 1985).

The second side of the debate is taken by some anthropologists who seek to explain female genital modifications from a scientific rather than political perspective. Anthropologists have been accused (see Daly, 1978; Hosken, 1976; Lyons, 1981) of "perpetuating a 'cover-up' of the dangerous and sexually disabling effects of clitoridectomy and infibulation." In my view, rather than perpetuate a cover-up, anthropologists working with African societies have sought instead to understand and explain female genital mutilations in terms of the cultural context in which they occur. Using this approach, genital modifications have been discussed in the context of the level of violence in societies, the degree of sexual interest, the status of women, and the structuring of social relations. Unfortunately, since there has been little systematic comparative research on genital modifications (and especially female ones), the state of our knowledge is accurately assessed by Gregerson (1982: 100): "Whatever the reason, people in many different societies have felt and still feel that the genitals should be altered in one way or another by cutting, piercing, hacking, or slicing or by inserting objects."

The third side to the debate is the viewpoint of the tribal peoples about the genital modifications they choose to perform or submit to. While there is no systematically collected data about the attitudes of tribal people in Africa and the Middle East, the information that does exist suggests that more often than not genital modifications are seen as a mark of ethnic identity that is more important than any pain or suffering that the operation may bring: (1) African women resisted the anticlitoridectomy initiative at the 1980 UN Conference on Women; (2) the Mau Mau rebellion in Kenya focused in part on families excluded from church schools because they failed to reject clitoridectomies; (3) Gusii women take pride in having the operation; (4) more Igbo women are having clitoridectomies and at an earlier age; and (5) in Nairobi, women from tribes in which clitoridectomies were not performed traditionally are now choosing to have them (Carlebach, 1962; LeVine, 1979; Lyons, 1981; Ottenberg, 1968). Of course, this third viewpoint does not necessarily conflict, at least in the scientific sense, with the antimodification position. It is reasonable to assume that tribal identity as reflected by a genital modification indicates identification with a

TABLE 5.2
Female Genital Modifications and Inequality

Society	1	2	3	4	5	6	7	8	9	10	11	12	13	14
Aranda	+	+	+	+	0	+	0	+	+	0	0	—	+	+
Luo	+	+	+	—	—	+	—	+	+	+	+	+	+	0
Dogon	—	0	—	—	—	—	—	+	+	+	—	—	—	—
Masai	+	—	—	—	+	+	—	+	+	+	—	—	—	—
Mossi	+	+	+	+	+	+	+	+	+	+	—	+	+	—
Somali	—	+	—	—	+	+	+	+	+	+	+	—	+	—
Hausa	+	0	+	+	—	+	—	—	+	—	—	—	+	—
Amhara	+	0	—	+	+	+	—	—	+	+	—	+	+	0
Zulu	—	0	—	+	0	+	+	+	+	+	—	—	+	—
Igbo	—	0	—	+	—	—	—	—	+	+	—	—	—	—

1 = wife-beating frequency
2 = wife-beating severity
3 = intervention
4 = female work groups
5 = female wealth
6 = property inheritance
7 = fruits of labor control
8 = widow remarriage freedom
9 = menstrual taboos
10 = dwelling ownership
11 = divorce freedom
12 = premarital sex double standard
13 = domestic authority
14 = infanticide sex preference

culture in which females are dominated by men and in which the modification also reflects that dominance.

While it is impossible to test the relationship between female genital modifications and sexual inequality with the data at hand, it is possible to provide a preliminary test as shown in Table 5.2. The plus sign indicates that the variable score supports a modification-inequality link, a minus sign that the score fails to support the link, and a zero that no data is available. For 8 of the 14 variables, the modification-inequality link is supported (wife-beating frequency, wife-beating severity, female work groups, property inheritance, widow remarriage freedom, menstrual taboos, dwelling ownership, and domestic authority). Thus there is some evidence tying female genital modifications to sexual inequality, a pattern I would expect to disappear as women's power and status increases and as ethnic identification weakens (McLean and Graham, 1982).

SUMMARY

The findings reported in this chapter indicate that it is too simplistic to argue that sexual inequality, in some broad, undefined form, causes wife beating. But, the findings also indicate that one form of sexual inequality—economic inequality—is a strong predictor of wife beating.

The link between economic inequality and wife beating is apparently mediated by two other factors. First, male dominance in family decision making; second, restrictions on female divorce freedom. A new model of sexual inequality and wife beating focusing on these factors is provided, with the hope that other researchers will test its trustworthiness with an independent cross-cultural sample. This chapter also provides evidence that some presumed causes of wife beating, such as a premarital double standard governing sexual behavior and patrilocal postmarital residence are unrelated to wife beating frequency.

-6-

PULLING THE PIECES TOGETHER

This chapter has three purposes. First, I will summarize the basic findings of this cross-cultural study as reported at length in the previous chapters. Second, I will review what these findings tell us about the cross-cultural validity of the theories and perspectives on family violence outlined in Chapter 1. And, third, I will synthesize the findings relevant to the causes of wife beating and the physical punishment of children, in order to provide a broad understanding of these two most common types of family violence.

BASIC CONCLUSIONS

Viewed in a broad, worldwide perspective, this study suggests seven major conclusions about family violence.

(1) While there is a seemingly endless variety of ways people will find to cause physical harm to members of their families, only a few forms of family violence occur commonly around the world. These are wife beating, physical punishment of children, and fighting between siblings. Not only do these forms of violence occur in many societies, but in a significant number they occur with considerable frequency. Other forms of family violence, such as infanticide, patricide, and killing of the aged, while leading to shocked reaction when they do occur, actually occur rarely, both intra- and interculturally.

(2) While no family member is entirely immune from family violence, adult women are most likely to be the victims while adult men are most likely to be the perpetrators and least likely to be the victims. In addition, women are more likely than any other category of family members to suffer severe and debilitating injuries. While these women usually suffer at the hands of their husbands, we should not overlook women in matrilocal societies who may be beaten by their brothers, and girls in Africa who suffer the lifelong effects of various genital operations. .

(3) Most people in the world at some point in their lives either experience or witness violence between members of their families. Most

people probably experience or witness violence while they are children: in 74% of societies children are physically punished by caretakers; in 44% of societies siblings fight with one another; and wife beating, which occurs in 84% of societies, is often more frequent in the early years of marriage when young children are present in the household.

(4) Wife beating and the physical punishment of children are the two most common types of family violence found throughout the world.

(5) Wife beating occurs more often in societies in which husbands have the economic and the ultimate decision making power in the household, and adults often resolve conflicts with other adults by fighting with one another.

(6) Physical punishment of children is most often a routine part of child rearing in societies at the high end of the scale of societal complexity.

(7) Violence is not an inevitable consequence of family life, as evidenced by the 16 societies, discussed in Chapter 7, in which family violence is largely nonexistent.

THEORETICAL PERSPECTIVES

In Chapter 1, I briefly outlined the nine theoretical perspectives that have guided much of the recent research on the causes of family violence. The purpose of this section is to review the findings of the research reported in the previous chapters in terms of what that research tells us about the trustworthiness of these theories.

Resource Theory

Resource theory suggests that power in marital relations is determined by the relative value of the resources each party brings to the marriage. As discussed in Chapter 5, there is considerable cross-cultural evidence that control of economic and organizational resources is a strong predictor of male dominance in many societies. The findings of this study suggest that the resource-control perspective also explains, at least in part, wife beating. Control of economic resources is a powerful direct predictor of male dominance in the family and a powerful indirect predictor of wife-beating frequency. Organizational resources, on the other hand, are not an especially powerful predictor of wife beating, although wife beating is somewhat more frequent in polygynous societies.

As regards status inconsistency theory, the cross-cultural data are not detailed enough to permit any conclusions about the effect of social change on male or female status or on wife beating.

Exchange Theory

Exchange theory suggests that male aggressiveness, isolation of the family, and sexual inequality create a social context in which husbands can get away with hitting their wives. The findings here suggest that economic inequality between men and women is a powerful predictor of wife beating. Male aggressiveness is also related to wife beating in one way, but not in another. In societies in which men are likely to settle conflicts with other men violently, wife beating is more common. But, hypermasculinity is weakly related to wife beating. Thus it seems that norms governing conflict resolution techniques are a more important predictor of wife beating than is aggressiveness resulting from the need to project a macho image. As for the third factor, social isolation, I find little evidence that social isolation is related to wife beating.

Thus at the cross-cultural level, the norms that allow men to hit their wives (and to keep the costs of doing so low) are economic inequality, as suggested by Gelles (1983), and violent conflict resolution.

Culture of Violence Theory

The findings here provide either no or only partial support for three hypotheses derived from the culture of violence framework. First, there is little evidence of a violence spillover effect—the presence of other forms of socially acceptable violence does not consistently predict either wife beating or the physical punishment of children. Second, the findings fail to support a strong link between aggressive male behavior and wife beating. Rather, it seems, in societies with high levels of male aggression, that aggression is more often aimed at targets outside the family. Third, the findings provide partial support for the general culture of violence model. While family violence is unrelated to violence directed at targets outside the society, it is related to violence between acquaintances and one form of family violence tends to be related to other forms. Last, it seems that spousal violence can profitably be conceptualized as a form of conflict resolution that tends to occur more often in societies in which disputes between adults are often settled violently.

Patriarchal Theory

The central premise of this study is that the concept of patriarchal society is too broad a notion for cross-cultural testing. Thus the strategy has been to define and conceptualize female status and power in very specific ways that are measurable with cross-cultural ethnographic data. When approached this way, it seems clear that there is no unidimensional relationship between female status and power and wife beating. Rather, some aspects of inequality, such as control of women's premarital sexual behavior and place of residence, are unrelated to wife beating while other aspects are related. Among the key inequality predictors of wife beating are male economic power in the family, male decision-making power in the family, and restrictions on the freedom of women to divorce their husbands. One of the basic findings of this study is that economic inequality strongly predicts wife beating. Another key finding is that women's economic power or solidarity with other women is a powerful predictor of the absence of wife beating.

Social Learning Theory

The social learning framework suggests that family violence is the product of the interaction of contextual and situational factors. When the findings of this study are viewed from this perspective, it is clear that there are contextual and situational factors that occur over and over again in societies around the world. The two basic contextual factors, as mentioned, are gender-based economic inequality and violent conflict resolution. The key situational factor is sexual jealousy on the part of the husband, which often precipitates a wife-beating incident. As regards physical punishment of children, the basic contextual factor seems to be a complex social order that requires obedient, compliant, and cooperative citizens who can follow orders, respect authority, and work together. Although the evidence is not clear and is discussed in more detail next, one key situational factor might be isolation of the family, which places an enormous child care responsibility on the mother.

The intergenerational transmission theory has been indirectly supported here, with each form of family violence generally associated with other forms. There is also anecdotal evidence for this theory, as the ethnographic record suggests that older siblings learn to care for younger siblings by imitating the child-rearing behavior of their parents.

Ecological Theory

The ecological perspective, with its emphasis on the social context of family violence, has important implications for this research, based as it is on societal-level data. Two of Garbarino's (1977) arguments concerning child abuse (redefined here as physical punishment of children) are supported. First, child punishment is linked to social isolation of the family, as indicated by less frequent use of physical punishment in extended-family households. Second, an absence of physical punishment is linked to appropriate expectations about children's behavior, as parents in many societies punish children only for behaviors that are beyond the bounds of what is considered acceptable at a certain age.

As regards Belsky's (1980) four-level model, there is some evidence here of an interaction between what occurs at the societal level and what occurs in the family setting. This is especially the case for both sexual economic inequality and violent conflict resolution in which societal norms effect behavior in the family.

Evolutionary Theory

As will be discussed later in this chapter, there does appear to be a link between societal complexity and more child punishment, and there is the possibility of an indirect link between complexity and more wife beating. Why societal complexity has such an effect is not yet clear; some possible explanations are set forth further along in the chapter.

Sociobiological Theory

Hypotheses based on parental certainty and sex ratio theory concerning child abuse and infanticide are not tested here. However, this does not mean that these ideas are not testable with cross-cultural data, just that this task is left to others.

General Systems Theory

The findings of this study as they relate to Straus's positive feedback model are summarized in Figure 6.1. I think it is important to focus on the model in its entirety because it brings together in one place nearly all of the factors that at one time or another have been mentioned as causes

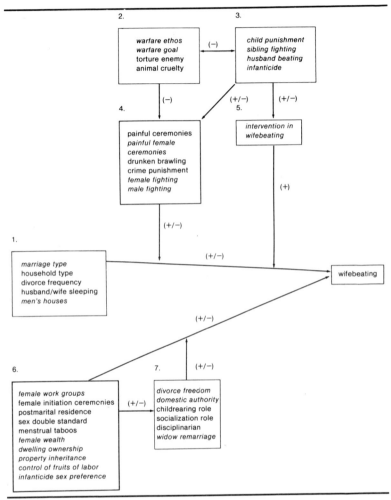

Figure 6.1. The Straus Model in Cross-Cultural Perspective.

of family violence. However, I do so with four major restrictions in mind. First, I have operationalized all the factors in the model at the societal level, though Straus clearly assumed that some of the factors operate at the family or interactional level. Thus my test results do not represent a full test of the model, at least not in the form that it was conceptualized by Straus. Second, I ignore the positive feedback nature of the model, and focus only on the presumed causal flow from left to right. Third, I am interested in the model only as an explanation for wife beating; as discussed previously, wife beating seems to be a separate phenomenon from the physical punishment of children and sibling fighting, and as such, requires a distinct explanation. Fourth, in fairness, Straus did not propose the model as an end-point, but as a starting point for those seeking to explain family violence.

The easiest way to discuss the model in cross-cultural context is to begin with the factors in box 1 and work through the boxes in order. A plus sign indicates that the cross-cultural relationship among the variables is as the model predicts, a minus sign indicates that the hypothesized relationship does not exist, and a plus/minus sign (+/–) indicates that the relationship exists for some factors but not others or that the predicted relationships exist but are weak. Factors that are italicized are those that seem to operate in the predicted fashion, at least in terms of their association with other factors.

Box 1 concerns a "high level of conflict inherent in the family." Its hypothesized direct link to wife beating is supported in part, as wife beating frequency is associated with polygynous marriage and the presence of men's houses. Box 2 concerns a "high level of violence in the society." This is usually seen as indirectly leading to wife beating through the factors in boxes 3 and 4. The cross-cultural evidence, however, suggests that the level of violence in a society, as measured by violence directed at other societies, has little relationship to family violence. Externally directed violence appears neither to encourage more violence in the family (box 3) nor to stimulate more interpersonal violence in general (box 4). The only relationship of note for box 2 is that between a societal ethos emphasizing warfare and men actively seeking to achieve status through heroism on the battlefield. But neither of these variables is directly or indirectly related to wife beating. Box 3 ("family socialization in violence") is also generally conceptualized as an indirect cause of wife beating, through box 4 (interpersonal violence) and 5 (norms legitimizing family violence). First, it is important to note that box 3 is the only box where all of the cluster factors are actually statistically associated with one another. As regards the links to other boxes, box 3 is inconsistently related to box 4 and weakly related to box 5. As regards the tie to box 4, 17 of the 24 possible realtionships between the factors are in the predicted direction, but only four have coefficients worth noting. The key factor seems to be painful initiation ceremonies for girls, which is related to child punishment, sibling fighting, and infanticide—and to wife beating as well.

Female and male fighting, which are also related to wife beating, are linked to husband beating but not to the other forms of family violence in box 3. As for the link between box 3 and 5, all the coefficients are positive, though weak. Thus, to sum up this complicated set of relationships involving boxes 2, 3, 4, 5, and wife beating, it seems that the model is supported in part as some indicators of interpersonal violence at the family and community level are related to one another and to wife beating frequency. However, as suggested earlier, there is no compelling cross-cultural evidence that there is any sort of direct, one-to-one relationship between the level of violence in a society beyond the family level and the level of violence in families in that society.

The lower half of the Straus model containing boxes 6 and 7 concerns the effect of sexual inequality on wife beating. Box 6 concerns sexual inequality at the societal level, while box 7 concerns sexual inequality in the family. As discussed in the previous chapter, economic inequality, male domestic authority, and restrictions on women's marital freedom are all aspects of sexual inequality that are linked both to one another and to wife-beating frequency. Thus this part of the Straus model is supported in part.

The Straus model in its full form provides a useful framework for identifying and unraveling the connections between variables that there is reason to believe may predict wife beating. The cross-cultural findings reported here suggest that a number of these factors are related to wife beating in the direction suggested by the model. However, the cross-cultural data also suggest that, at least at the societal level of analysis, the model is too complex. While my operationalization of the model posits 7 boxes and 36 variables, the analysis in the previous chapters and other theoretical perspectives suggest that far fewer boxes and variables are needed to account for family violence around the world. The purpose of the remainder of the chapter is to reconsider some of the findings reported here in order to arrive at a streamlined explanation for family violence.

SEXUAL INEQUALITY, VIOLENCE, AND WIFE BEATING

Figure 6.2 is a diagram of the sexual inequality-conflict resolution model of wife beating suggested by the research reported here. Of course, this model is preliminary and subject to revision or rejection following future testing with a new cross-cultural sample of societies. The model combines the four sets of factors that are the strongest predictors of frequent wife beating in societies around the world—sexual economic inequality, violent conflict resolution, male domestic authority, and divorce restrictions for women. When these four conditions are present in a society and in families, the likelihood is

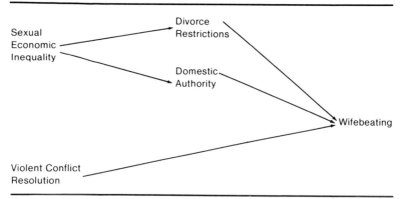

Figure 6.2. Inequality—Conflict Model of Wife Beating.

TABLE 6.1

Relationships Among Inequality—Conflict Model Variables

	1	2	3	4	5	6	7	8	9
(1) Property inheritance		.30*	.23	.31*	.29*	.29*	.15	−.12	.12
(2) Fruits of labor			.37*	.27*	.20	.57*	.07	.11	.25*
(3) Female wealth				.19	.07	.39*	.15	−.10	.22
(4) House ownership					.33*	.31*	.36*	.05	.22
(5) Divorce freedom						.13	.13	.09	.24*
(6) Domestic authority							.02	−.10	.45*
(7) Male fighting								.38*	.34*
(8) Female fighting									.25*
(9) Wife beating frequency									

*Significant at .05 level.

strong that wife beating will occur in a majority of households in the society. And, while it is clear that each of the factors is associated with frequent wife beating, it is also clear (as shown by the correlations reported in Tables 6.1 and 6.2) that the combined effect of these factors is stronger yet. The partial tau correlations reported in Table 6.2 indicate that when the influence of any one factor is controlled, the relationship between the other factor and wife beating is weaker. For example, the tau coefficient between male domestic authority and wife beating is .64. This coefficient is reduced to .39 when female fighting is controlled, .46 when male fighting is controlled, and .40 when divorce freedom is controlled. The same pattern holds for the other factors. Thus the central conclusion of this study as regards the cause of wife beating is that wife beating is more likely to occur and more likely to be frequent in societies in which men control the family wealth and adults

TABLE 6.2
Partial Tau Correlations for Inequality—Conflict Model

wife beating × domestic authority (female fighting)	.39
wife beating × domestic authority (male fighting)	.46
wife beating × domestic authority (divorce freedom)	.40
wife beating × divorce freedom (domestic authority)	.21
wife beating × divorce freedom (female fighting)	.23
wife beating × divorce freedom (male fighting)	.20
wife beating × male fighting (domestic authority)	.32
wife beating × male fighting (divorce freedom)	.23
wife beating × female fighting (domestic violence)	.29
wife beating × female fighting (divorce freedom)	

often solve conflicts by resorting to physical violence. The effect of male control of family wealth seems to be indirect in that control of wealth affords men power in family decision making and restricts the freedom of wives to obtain a divorce.

There are a number of societies in our sample that display the pattern shown in Figure 6.2, but perhaps the Rundi of Burundi in central Africa provide the clearest example. The description that follows is based largely on Ethel Albert's (1963) study of Rundi women.

Rundi society is traditionally described as patriarchial with a high value placed on power, authority, and the possession of material wealth, and with considerable individual concern over one's place in the social hierarchy. The Rundi social order is one of the more highly complex and stratified in our sample, as evidenced by the presence of castes and social classes and individual status distinctions based on family background, sex, and age.

Rundi society is divided into three castes. At the top are the 10% of the population in the Tutsi caste who are primarily cattle herders. Below them are the 85% of the population in the Hutu caste who are primarily farmers and farmer-herders. The lowest caste, the Twa are primarily potters and hunters and are considered to be much inferior to the other two. Within each caste are smaller patrilineal social divisions arranged hierarchically, like social classes. Within the patrilineages are the families (nuclear and polygynous) that are also ordered hierarchically, with the father as the head and his wife or wives and children owing "him respect and obedience." Sons inherit the valuable family property and livestock from their fathers, while daughters inherit household and personal possessions from their mothers. Daughters marry out of the household, but always maintain allegiance to their fathers and respect for their authority.

While individuals remain for life in the caste into which they are born, the social hierarchy is flexible and individuals can improve their position. This flexibility comes from each person occupying a number of different status positions at one time. Thus, for example, a Tutsi woman is inferior to her father and her husband, an equal and competitor with co-wives, and a superior to Hutu men and women. Throughout their lives, the Rundi also have ample opportunity to increase their individual or family status, either through marriage or the acquisition of additional wealth, and individual Rundi may add to their power and prestige throughout their lifetimes. While a woman's wealth and status is often a function of her husband's, Rundi women of independent wealth and power are not unheard of, and some Rundi widows choose not to remarry so that they can retain some of their husband's wealth for themselves.

In general, women are considered to be the inferior of men: "Woman, says the proverb, is only the passive earth; it is the man who provides the seed" (Albert, 1963: 192). Women are considered better suited for physical labor, less agile, less courageous, more easily frustrated, more emotional, and likely to age more quickly. Women bear the major responsibility for food preparation, household chores and child rearing, and, while expected to defer to their husbands on most matters, control the distribution of food to the family. There is evidently some difference between Tutsi and Hutu families in who dominates in the household. In Hutu households, the man is clearly in charge, but in Tutsi households the wife may enjoy considerable power, although Tutsi husbands vehemently deny this. Divorce is frequent and "a young woman lives like a nomad" moving from her father's home to her husband's, back to her father's, back to her husband's, back to her father's, off to her second husband's, and so on (Albert, 1963: 203). Husbands and wives can both seek divorce, although men have a longer list of reasons that justify such action, including a wife's disobedience or laziness, sterility, or her speaking against him in public.

Husbands have the right to beat their wives and fathers the right to beat their children:

> For, physical violence is the privilege of the superior. It is up to him to instruct and correct his inferiors by words and blows. Or, if he is in a bad humour, his inferiors are always around, and he can take out his displeasure on them. Children expect to be beaten by their parents, serfs and servants by their master and mistress, and a woman, even an *imfura*, considers it quite normal for her husband to beat her, especially if she has been difficult or if he has had a good deal to drink [Albert, 1963: 190].

As suggested by this quote, conflict and violence are far from unknown in Rundi social relations. In fact, it is the absence of conflict that is unusual:

However, neighbors, acquaintances, relatives, and spouses, it is said, do not remain friendly for a very long time. Several months, at most two or three years, suffice to create reasons for hatred, jealousy, vengeance, burning a house, calumny, fights, and visits to the witch to obtain poison [Albert 1963: 191].

To a large extent, violence among the Rundi arises from two sources. First, from competition between equals for access to increased wealth or status. Second, from the hierarchical social order that is maintained in part by norms that enable superiors to use violence to control inferiors.

As the foregoing description indicates, the Rundi social order displays many of the factors associated with frequent wife beating: male control of wealth, male dominance in the home, violent conflict resolution, and easier divorce for husbands than for wives, although women can and do get divorces on their own. The Rundi also display one other social feature that we have not yet considered in detail, though it may be predictive of family violence—a rigidly structured social hierarchy that clearly delineates superiors and inferiors, and gives superiors control over the lives of inferiors, whatever the basis of that inferior status (sex, age, caste, wealth, and so on).

Since a structured social order and status distinctions are characteristic of socially and politically complex societies, the Rundi situation suggests that social complexity may have something to do with the frequency of wife beating, just as it does with the physical punishment of children. As we saw earlier, social complexity is not directly related to the frequency of wife beating, although it may be indirectly related through its effects on the economic inequality and conflict resolution norms. This interpretation is suggested by the earlier findings of Whyte (1978) and Zelman (1974) who report that social complexity in their cross-cultural samples is related to female control of property and to female power. However, in both of these studies the correlation coefficients are weak and somewhat inconsistent, making it difficult to draw any firm conclusions about the relationship between social complexity and economic sexual inequality.

My data does not make the picture much clearer. The three measures of complexity used here—population size, degree of dependence on agriculture, and intensity of agriculture—show only weak or negative relationships to the four economic inequality and two conflict resolution variables. Thus at this point the only reasonable conclusion we can reach is that there is no evidence to suggest that social complexity in a general sense is either directly or indirectly associated with wife beating.

However, the Rundi situation suggests that the hierarchical social ordering that accompanies social complexity may encourage wife beating if two sets of norms and values are also present. First, there are norms that legitimate the classification of certain individuals or groups as superiors and certain other individuals or groups as inferiors. This set of norms must be accompanied by the shared belief that the superiors have the inherent right to control the lives of the inferiors. Second, there are norms that encourage upward social mobility, especially through competition between individuals or groups that occupy equal status positions in the social hierarchy. When these two sets of norms are present in a hierarchically ordered social structure, the Rundi case suggests that we would expect to find violent conflict resolution and economic sexual inequality and frequent wife beating. However, in the absence of these two sets of norms, social complexity may have no influence on the frequency of wife beating, as evidenced by the situation among the Central Thai, as described in detail in the following chapter.

Obviously, all of this is conjecture at this point, with the relationship between social complexity and wife beating requiring further, more careful cross-cultural study. A major goal and a major problem for future cross-cultural research on this issue is how to define and measure variables meaningfully, such as social mobility, superiority-inferiority, and competition for status with the limited cross-cultural data available in the ethnographic record. While the task is not an easy one, it is by no means impossible, as suggested by Justinger's (1978) success in collecting data on the perceptions and realities of social mobility in 60 societies around the world.

PHYSICAL PUNISHMENT OF CHILDREN

Unlike wife beating and husband beating, this study has produced few new insights into cross-cultural variations and patterns in the use of physical punishment in child rearing. There have been few new insights because we already know a fair amount about child rearing in cross-cultural perspective. We know, for example, that physical punishment is used in a vast majority of societies around the world. We also know that physical punishment is more likely to be used in societies with mother-child households than in societies with nuclear or extended-family households. And we know that physical punishment will more often be an accepted part of child rearing in more complex societies. These basic conclusions suggested by a dozen or more cross-cultural studies cited earlier have all been confirmed by the analysis here. Two of these conclusions—the links between child punishment and household composition and complex social organization—require further discussion.

I have found little evidence to support the contention that nuclear family households are associated with frequent use of physical punishment, and similarly for wife beating. Wathan (n.d.) has reached a similar conclusion with the Standard Cross-Cultural Sample; she finds no relationship between pain infliction on children and household organization. What does seem to be true cross-culturally is that children are more likely to be physically punished in societies in which there are large numbers of single-parent households. And most of these societies tend to have some polygynous marriages in which the single-parent households are generally composed of a co-wife and her children. Since polygynous family relationships are subject to all sorts of rivalries, jealousies, and conflicts, it is not at all surprising that mothers should resort to physical punishment, both as a means to keep their children in line and as a way of venting their own frustrations and rage. (Societies with polygynous households also tend to have more wife beating and fighting between co-wives.)

It is important to note that while nuclear family households are not the scene of frequent family violence in the societies sampled here, it is possible that nuclear family households in modern, complex societies are an arena for family violence. As Straus and others have suggested for some years, it may be the isolation of the nuclear family and the associated high level of interaction among family members in nuclear families that leads to family violence. This specific proposition is not testable with the available cross-cultural data, although my impression is that nuclear families in small-scale societies are less isolated than are those in more complex societies. This impression supports the proposition that it is the degree of isolation and the level of interaction, not the type of family alone, that predicts the level of family violence.

Turning now to the link between societal complexity and physical punishment of children, Petersen et al. (1982) suggest that parents in economically and politically complex societies are often much concerned about raising compliant, conforming children. Petersen and his associates reason that since parents in complex societies often must conform to supervision, they are likely to encourage conformity in their children, especially by means of physical punishment. Their path analysis supports this interpretation, as does my analysis that shows a gamma of .454 between physical punishment and the degree to which a society depends on agriculture for food production. This pattern and the possible influence of household type becomes clearer when we divide the sample societies into three groups based on type of household and degree of dependence on agriculture, using the *Ethnographic Atlas* (Murdock, 1967) codes for dependence on agriculture: (1) societies with nuclear family households and less than 55% dependence on agriculture for food; (2) societies with nuclear family households and over 55% dependence on agriculture; and (3) societies with nonnuclear family households and over 55% dependence on agriculture.

The mean scores for these three groups for use of physical punishment are 1.81 for group 1 (n = 22), 2.44 for group 2 (n = 18), and 2.68 for group 3 (n = 22). I assume that the high score for group 3 is in part the result of classifying societies with polygynous, single-parent households in this category. However, the fact that groups 2 and 3 are considerably higher on physical punishment than is group 1 suggests that economic complexity, as reflected in subsistence practices, is a predictor of physical punishment; household type, other than polygynous single-parent, is of relatively little importance. It seems quite clear that the more complex the society, the more likely children will be physically punished. However, while it easy to talk about the separate or mutual effects of household type and societal complexity on the use of physical punishment, the relationships are much less clear when we focus on a single society or community. When we narrow our focus in this way, it is often not clear whether it is the societally imposed need to raise compliant children or the isolation of the nuclear family that leads parents to use physical punishment. A case in point is the community of Rocky Roads in rural Jamaica as described by Yehudi Cohen (1966).

Cohen provides us with a rich and detailed description of life in the 57 households that make up the rural community of Rocky Roads. Actually, to describe Rocky Roads as a community somewhat overstates the case:

> Rocky Roads is composed of isolated, independent nuclear families. There is no inter-household discipline and control nor is there any mechanism for the pooling of resources between households or any such similar social units [Cohen, 1966: 2].

Despite the isolation of the households, Rocky Roaders live within the wider Jamaican political and economic system. They vote in local and national elections, although who they vote for seems of little concern. There is a local church. The government provides a local agricultural agent and collects land taxes. The children attend school. Adolescent girls often go off to the cities to work. There are clearly distinguishable low, middle, and upper classes in the community, based on the widely shared criteria of individual wealth and skin color (lighter skin brings higher status). And, most importantly, there is the Saturday trip to the parish market to sell to the English townsfolk the yams, sweet potatoes, Irish potatoes, corn, bananas, eggs, poultry, and livestock the villagers grow and raise.

The family division of labor means that men spend most of their days in the fields while women spend their time at home tending to their gardens, managing the household, and caring for the children. A Rocky Road infant's life revolves around his or her mother—"His home is his world and the world's representative his mother" (Cohen, 1966: 40). During infancy the father, though physically present, "is neither a gratifying nor a punishing person" (Cohen, 1966: 59). The major goals of infant socialization are to break infants of their natural tendency to be aggressive and to protect them from evil spirits.

These goals are achieved primarily by physical punishment—first, by slaps with an open hand, and then, when infants begin to walk, by floggings for getting in their mothers' way, for crying for no good reason, for destroying their mothers' property, for disobeying, for taking another's food, and so on.:

> There are two kinds of flogging. One is with a strap; the other is with a switch, a small but strong and flexible branch of a tree, which produces a shrill whistle when swung. Infants in Rocky Roads are flogged with switches. When a mother flogs her infant child she holds on to him with one hand and administers the flogging with the other to the little one's bottom. Floggings are very effective; little girls wear short dresses and little boys wear only shirts. "If you don't hit your child when he is young," say the people of Rocky Roads, "he gets hard, and you cannot bend him as you would like to bend him" [Cohen, 1966: 57].

Childhood begins between the ages of 5 and 7. The strap replaces the switch and floggings become more severe and more patterned. But children have learned by now that by running and hiding until their parent's temper cools, they can often avoid a flogging. Children are also punished by confinement to a room or by being made to eat alone after the family completes its meal. However, children are never made to miss a meal as "This is a form of sadism which Rocky Roaders consider quite inhuman" (Cohen, 1966: 59). In childhood, the father plays an active role, primarily as the principal disciplinarian who administers floggings for serious offenses of the day upon his arrival home from the fields. Extensive use of floggings, the threat of floggings, and other punishments are consistent with the continuing goal of rearing offspring who are compliant and dependent:

> Anything—and we are being carefully deliberate and literal in our usages—which a child does without direction by the mother brings on the criticism of rudeness. The ideal child is the docile one who remains unobtrusively seated in one spot without attracting any attention and without making any demands, especially for food. . . . The thwarting of independent behavior which begins in infancy increases in intensity

during childhood. Rocky Roads socialization is restrictive in the strictest sense of the word [Cohen, 1966: 64].

Once they reach adolescence, boys are given a piece of land by their fathers to farm; they may also work on others' land or on their fathers' land. From their earnings they must pay room and board to their parents, buy their own clothing, and save as much as possible toward the goal of purchasing more land for themselves. Floggings by his father still continue, but a boy's own physical strength and his economic contribution to the family afford him some protection, except when he is in serious violation of some parental order. For boys who fail to make the expected economic contribution, threat of expulsion from the household becomes the most powerful punishment.

Adolescent girls who remain at home continue to live under the control of their mothers. Many girls, however, choose to go to the towns or the city where they use their household skills as domestic helpers. These girls have considerable freedom and few obligations to their family.

As the situation among the Rocky Roaders suggests, it is not easy to pinpoint what specific factors lead parents in a particular society or community to use physical punishment with their children. For Rocky Roads, the isolation of the nuclear families and the child care burden placed on the mothers are consistent with the proposition that the stress associated with raising children without assistance leads to the use of physical punishment. But at the same time, the Rocky Roads experience is also consistent with the proposition that compliance is an adaptive personality trait in complex societies with hierarchical social systems. There is little doubt that Rocky Roads girls will be more economically successful as housekeepers if they are compliant and cooperative and that boys will amass more wealth if they can work for other landowners and satisfy their fathers. Thus in Rocky Roads, we can see how forces operating at the societal level and forces operating at the family level mesh to encourage the use of physical punishment in child rearing. Whether this pattern holds for all societies or for some specific types of societies is by no means clear and is a crucial question for future cross-cultural research.

-7-

PREVENTION AND CONTROL

This chapter takes us full circle. In Chapter 2, I listed and described the types of family violence found in societies throughout the world. In Chapters 3 through 6, I presented the results of our tests of various hypotheses developed to explain family violence. Here, I describe the means societies use to try to control and prevent family violence in their midst. I approach this topic in two ways. First, I focus on the prevention and control of wife beating because wife beating is the most common form of family violence around the world and, as such, is the subject of more public concern than are other types of family violence. Thus in most societies, more effort is devoted to controlling wife beating than, for example, controlling physical punishment of children, which is seen as primarily the caretaker's business, or husband beating which is seen as relatively harmless. This situation is somewhat the reverse of that in the United States where the laws governing the reporting and prevention of child abuse and neglect are more stringently enforced than are those governing wife beating. Perhaps this is because the physical punishment of children and child abuse and neglect is more common in the United States than is wife beating, which is, again, the reverse of the pattern displayed by most of the societies sampled here. Second, I analyze the 16 societies in our sample in which family violence of any kind is virtually nonexistent. The goal here is to produce a list of sociocultural traits that are predictive of the absence of family violence.

WIFE-BEATING INTERVENTIONS

In Table 7.1, I list the six major types of interventions used in societies around the world. The second column in the table lists the number of societies in which that intervention is the primary one used; the third column lists the number of societies in which that intervention is of secondary importance.

The six interventions are scaled from low to high on the basis of the immediacy of their use to control a wife-beating incident. Thus Type I—immediate intervention by relatives or neighbors—serves to break

TABLE 7.1
Wife-Beating Interventions

Intervention Type	No. of Societies Primary Type	No. of Societies Secondary Type
I. Immediate intervention by kin, neighbor or mediator	12	3
II. Wife given shelter by kin or neighbors	11	7
III. Public censure of husband by gossip, judicial proceeding, supernatural sanction, payment of compensation	11	7
IV. Wife can divorce husband	9	11
V. Intervention of one or more of above types only if beating is defined as too severe or for an inappropriate reason	19	1
VI. Intervention doesn't occur	6	—

up a beating in progress, while Type IV—divorce-occurs some time after a beating actually stops. Interventions I and II are what Bowker (1983) classifies as informal help, and are analogous to intervention by relatives, neighbors, friends, or the use of shelters in the United States. Interventions III and IV are formal sources of help and are analogous to intervention by police or the use of the court system, members of the clergy, or women's support groups in the United States. Of course, all of these interventions, whether formal or informal, represent tertiary prevention, as the major goal is to assist the wife (Goldstein, 1983).

Bowker (1983) reports from his Milwaukee study that formal interventions, interestingly, are more effective in stopping wife beating than are informal ones. Our findings are just the opposite, perhaps reflecting the frequent use of informal social control mechanisms in the societies in our sample. The intervention scale is highly correlated with both frequency of wife beating (rho = .51) and the severity of wife beating (rho = .32). The lesson here is that immediate intervention designed to stop the beating or to prevent it from ever starting is a key first line of defense in controlling wife beating. When neighbors or relatives or mediators jump in quickly to break up verbal or physical battles or to provide the wife with shelter, wife beating does not occur in many families. But, when the wife must wait for a judicial hearing or other public relief or when help arrives only when the beating goes too far, wife beating occurs in many families.

Just how do these interventions work in the real world? Among the Ona of the Tierra del Fuego, Types I and II serve to keep wife beating confined to a small minority of marriages.

Almost always it is the rough treatment on the part of the husband that drives his wife out of the hut. If he scolds or beats her and she herself has proved to be a compatible or industrious person, then her father or uncle or relative mediates with the husband; if he nevertheless does not change his behavior, they now advise the harassed women to simply flee [Gusinde, 1931: 344].

The Mossi of Upper Volta rely on a combination of Types II and III.

When a woman felt that she was being maltreated by her husband, she usually fled to her own patrilineage and waited for her husband's patrilineage—usually his brothers—to visit her male relatives and discuss the case. If the woman was judged guilty, she was reprimanded and sometimes flogged by her own relatives for causing trouble between the two lineages, and then sent home to her husband. However, if the man was found guilty, his wife was returned to him, but he was warned that he would lose all rights to her if he maltreated her again [Skinner, 1964: 79].

Among settled peasant societies such as the Mam of Guatemala, hearings can take a more formal form.

All civil disputes which are not settled by the families concerned come before the *Alcalde*. . . . There are many charges of adultery and of wife-beating. Either the wronged husband or the wife may go to the *Alcalde* to make a charge. Then the *Alcalde* sends the *mayores*, or even the *regidores*, to bring the accused spouse before him. . . . The proof of wife-beating is always the bruises [Wagley, 1941: 98].

And, Type III interventions can be quite informal, such as the talk of Igbo women in Nigeria.

Onitsha women are famous for their articulate and venomous tongues, and once a husband becomes known for tyranny he will be publicly gossiped about in the market, and humiliated [Henderson and Henderson, 1966: 12].

The data in Table 7.1 suggest that divorce is the most commonly used control for wife beating, although perhaps it is used as a last resort more often than are other types of control. Unfortunately, while divorce will end wife beating in a given marriage by ending the marital relationship, it apparently has little effect on the frequency or severity of wife beating in the society as a whole.

Table 7.1 also suggests that interventions are sometimes not used until the beating gets out of control. In these societies with Type V interventions, there is no control over beatings, per se, but only over ones that are culturally defined as excessive or unreasonable. This pattern is demonstrated by the Kapauku of New Guinea.

Although a husband may punish his wife even by wounding her or, for a serious offense such as adultery, by killing her, his position never approximates that of a tyrant. . . . Should he be harsh, unjust, or too emotional, his wife can always leave him and get a divorce even without the support of her relatives [Pospisil, 1958: 58].

Finally, we come to those six societies in which there is no intervention, as among the Southern Ojibwa.

But most marriages are fairly short and very stormy. Spouses kick and beat one another, use abusive language, desert one another, and, if they choose, reunite. Since each household is independent of every other, no one has the right to interfere with the course of marital relations [Landes, 1937: 104].

These few examples selected from dozens in the ethnographic literature reviewed for this book suggest that, when viewed cross-culturally, there is a large and varied arsenal of informal and formal mechanisms that can be used to control wife beating. Those that seem most effective—those that are used in societies in which wife beating is absent or rare—are ones that provide immediate protection for the wife. After-the-fact protection, while perhaps removing a wife from an abusive situation, does not seem to prevent wife beating in any general sense.

Perhaps the most important question raised by the variety of interventions found in societies around the world is why some societies use some interventions while other societies prefer other types. In the absence of any general theory to answer this question, the best approach seems to be to examine the relationship between intervention types and the sociocultural factors I have found to be related to wife beating. The results of the statistical analysis are reported in Table 7.2.

The results indicate that those factors that predict wife beating also predict the delayed use of interventions (Types IV and V) and the absence of intervention. It seems clear that battered wives will have less chance of receiving outside help in societies in which they have little economic power, in societies in which the husband rules the home, in societies in which they will have difficulty obtaining a divorce, and in societies in which disputes tend to be settled violently. This pattern of findings suggests that these tertiary interventions, in and of themselves, have little impact on controlling or preventing family violence at either the community or societal level. Rather, it seems that tertiary interventions are linked to low rates of wife beating because both the low rates and the interventions are part of a general pattern of male-female equality and nonviolent conflict resolution. The message here is that

TABLE 7.2
Intervention and Predictors of Wife Beating

Variable	
Female work groups	.217
Independent female wealth	.225
Female property inheritance	.186
Control of fruits of labor	.275*
Domestic decision making	.471*
Type of marriage	.392*
Divorce freedom	.185
Painful female initiation ceremonies	.414*
Female fighting	.131
Male fighting	.241

*Significant at .05 level.

tertiary approaches alone will not end wife beating and must be used in combination with primary approaches that focus on the underlying sociocultural causes of wife beating such as economic inequality.

SOCIETIES WITHOUT FAMILY VIOLENCE

As pointed out in Chapter 1, one of the major benefits of the cross-cultural comparative approach is that it enables us to examine ways of life that are different from our own. I rely on the comparative approach here to help provide us with a sociocultural profile of societies in which family life is free of violence. In Table 7.3, I list the 16 societies in our sample that are relatively free of family violence. Freedom from family violence is indicated by the family violence scale score in the second column of the table. This score, which ranges from 1.00 to 3.66, indicates the combined level of wife beating, husband beating, physical punishment of children, and sibling fighting that occurs in each society in the sample. Societies with a score of 1.00 have no or rare family violence.

These 16 societies provide an interesting subsample of the full 90-society sample on which this book is based. The 16 are representative of all seven major geographical regions of the world. However, South America is overrepresented with four societies (Ona, Siriona, Pemon, and Toba), while Africa (Bushmen) and Asia (Andamans and Central Thai) are underrepresented. Similarly, a broad range of economic systems (hunter-gatherers, horticulturalists, herders, agriculturalists) are covered, but hunter-gatherers (Ona, Andamans, Siriono, Bushmen)

TABLE 7.3
Societies Without Family Violence

	FVS	1	2	3	4	5	6	7	8	9
Fox	1.25	2	*3*	*3*	1	1	*5*	1	1	2
Iroquois	1.00	2	2	2	1	1	*4*	1	1	—
Papago	1.25	2	2	2	*2*	*2*	3	3	1	1
Ona	1.00	2	2	1	1	1	1	3	*3*	1
Siriono	1.25	*3*	—	*4*	1	1	1	—	1	1
Pemon	1.20	2	2	2	1	1	1	—	—	2
Toba	1.25	2	—	2	1	1	*4*	—	1	—
Javanese	1.25	1	1	2	1	*2*	3	1	1	1
Ifugao	1.00	2	2	*4*	1	1	3	—	2	*4*
Trobriands	1.33	2	2	2	1	1	3	2	1	2
Bushmen	1.00	*3*	2	2	1	1	1	—	1	1
Andamans	1.33	2	2	2	1	1	1	1	2	1
Central Thai	1.00	2	2	2	1	1	3	4	1	2
Kurd	1.33	2	*3*	*3*	1	1	—	—	1	1
L. Bedouin	1.00	2	*3*	2	1	*2*	1	3	2	—
Lapps	1.33	1	*3*	2	1	1	1	—	1	1

fvs = family violence scale
1 = domestic decision making
2 = control of fruits of family labor
3 = divorce freedom
4 = type of marriage

5 = premarital sex double standard
6 = divorce frequency
7 = intervention type
8 = male fighting
9 = husband/wife sleeping

NOTE: Italicized codes deviate from the typical pattern across these societies.

are overrepresented, perhaps because hunter-gatherers rarely mistreat their children (Rohner, 1986).

The nine columns of numbers in the table are the ratings for nine factors that seem especially typical of societies without family violence (italicized codes are ones that deviate from the typical pattern across these societies). In general, it seems that in societies without family violence, husbands and wives share in domestic decision making, wives have some control over the fruits of family labor, wives can divorce their husbands as easily as their husbands can divorce them, marriage is monogamous, there is no premarital sex double standard, divorce is relatively infrequent, husbands and wives sleep together, men resolve disputes with other men peacefully, and intervention in wife beating incidents tends to be immediate. Some of these findings are as I would expect, since they are simply the reverse of our findings regarding the causes of family violence. One should not be surprised, for example, to find that shared decision making in the household predicts the absence of wife beating since we already know that male dominance in decision making predicts wife beating. However, some of these findings do not follow this pattern, and, in fact, our earlier analysis indicated that they were unrelated to family violence. The three factors of interest in this regard—premarital double standard, the divorce rate, and husband-wife sleeping—are especially significant since they suggest that equality and closeness in the marital relationship lead to low rates of family violence. The central conclusion I reach from these findings is that family violence does not occur in societies in which family life is characterized by cooperation, commitment, sharing and equality. While these factors do not ensure that wives will not be beaten or children physically punished, it is clear that if they guide family relationships, family violence will be less frequent.

It should be noted, however, that some factors have been left out of the table because they seem to predict the absence of only one form of violence and have little or even an adverse effect on other forms. The best example of this class of factors is household organization, with extended-family households associated with the nonphysical punishment of children but unrelated to wife beating. Thus while it is possible, as I have done here, to produce a list of sociocultural characteristics of a family violence-free society, these factors, as a group, may be of limited predictive value when applied to a specific form of family violence.

THE CENTRAL THAI

It seems fitting to close by traveling to the Far East to describe the Central Thai, a society free of family violence. The Central Thai are a group of some 10 million people who speak the Central Thai dialect, live in central and southern Thailand, and are predominantly of the Buddhist faith. About 85% of the Central Thai live in rural communities where they grow rice for their own consumption and for cash sale. Our focus here is one of those rural agricultural communities—Bang Chan—a village of about 1,700 people about an hour's travel from Bangkok by road or three hours by canal. We know a great deal about Bang Chan because it was the focus of intensive study by teams of researchers from Cornell University. The information presented here is taken primarily from Phillips's (1966) *Thai Peasant Personality*.

Life in Bang Chan is much like life in hundreds of other Central Thai communities except that the proximity to Bangkok has made Bang Chaners more comfortable with urban ways and more reliant on some of the conveniences and pleasures of modern life. The 1,771 Bang Chaners live in some 296 distinct households. The majority of households are nuclear (59%), although a variety of extended-family arrangements (35%) are also common. Both men and women have much freedom in choosing mates. Marriages tend toward the unstable, with divorce considered justifiable for virtually any reason and preferred to remaining in a marriage filled with discord and conflict. Flexibility governs household living arrangements and many nuclear families often have an extra relative or two as members. Some families are also without the husband/father who may spend as much as six months each year working in Bangkok. The basic rule is that people can live together so long as they all get along peacefully and each does his or her share. Bang Chan families are remarkable for their absence of any meaningful division of labor by sex.

> In contrast to all other known cultures, in Thailand both men and women serve equally as midwives and do plowing. They both own and operate farms, inherit property equally, share equally in the property brought to a marriage and divide it equally in the case of divorce. It is not uncommon to find men tending babies while women are off on a business deal; nor is it unusual, as indicated earlier, to see women paddling right along with men as crew members in a boat race [Phillips, 1966: 82].

Individualism is a basic value in Bang Chan "1,771 individualists—polite, gentle, nonaggressive, but nevertheless individualists—pursuing their own purposes" (Phillips, 1966). Equally strong is a basic respect for others: "every individual regardless of his position in the hierarchy, deserves respect. The first is respect associated with the proper performance of one's role; the second, a recognition of the essential dignity of every human being." Along with individualism and mutual respect goes a strong need to control overt signs of aggression: "Because the volatility of a dispute is what is often most feared, one rarely hears of any actual argument accompanying the disagreement; instead, villagers say, 'We had a few words and he left. That's all.'"

This need to control aggressive feeling governs family relationships as well.

> Parents trying to come to terms with, or overcome, his preordained characteristics by inculcating good habits through example, coaxing, and whipping (the three modes of socialization, in order of priority, although villagers are more prone to talk about whippings than actually give them; most are too tenderhearted, and the rare whipping is almost always the result of sudden rage).

> Other than in horseplay, children do not push each other around; in my twenty-two months in Thailand, I saw not one case of young children in a serious fight, despite the fact that I looked for it. Very rare indeed is the parent who uses force or the threat of force on his child; there is no

Siamese equivalent of the American intimidation, "You had better do that or else . . ."

In another place, this same informant says of his relationship with his wife: "My wife and I never quarrel. If we quarreled, we would have to separate" [Phillips, 1966: 34, 35, 185].

While physical violence is rare in Bang Chan, the emotions that lead to violence in so many other societies are also felt by Bang Chaners. How do they deal with these feelings? Mainly by expressing them indirectly. Gossip is rampant, in fact so rampant and so predictable that it serves to resolve old conflicts rather than lead to new ones. People often flee from conflict-prone encounters, giggle in the face of awkward requests, are self-effacing, and use humor to smooth rough situations. And Bang Chaners express hostility in what we would call passive-aggressive ways. They sometimes steal another's property and return it only after the victim has shown sufficient concern over his loss to make the perpetrator feel better. And last, men will occasionally make public suicide attempts by hanging, which inevitably fail.

Many of the households are isolated in the center of wet rice fields, connected to one another and the local Buddhist monastery and government school by a series of canals. Other households are strung along the banks of major canals. As suggested by the desire to avoid conflict as just described, community relations are governed to a large extent by the belief that "if people live far away from each other, there will not be any trouble." This isolation, combined with the division of Bang Chan into nine administrative units by the Thai government, reflects an absence of any strong sense of community identity by the Bang Chaners. While they all feel mutual ties based on loyalty to the local monastery and school, and there are ambiguously defined kin groups beyond the family, the community can be described only as "loosely structured."

There are some important lessons in the Central Thai way of life for preventing family violence. Actually, it is somewhat surprising to be able to say this, as the Bang Chan community displays many of the sociocultural features commonly assumed to be tied to high levels of family violence. Bang Chaners live in isolated nuclear family households. Husbands may be away from the home for extended periods of time. The divorce rate is high. Household composition is unstable. And individuality is more important than is a shared sense of community identity. This could be a description of many communities in the contemporary United States as well as Bang Chan. But unlike the United States, family violence does not exist in Bang Chan. Why the difference? Three Bang Chan psychosocial patterns seem most important: first, the goal of avoiding disputes and the range of nonviolent techniques available to deal with aggressive feelings; second, the basic respect Bang Chaners have for one another, based on the belief that all people are entitled to such respect regardless of their role, status, or power; and third, and most important, the virtual absence of a division of labor by sex in the household. To a large extent, there is no men's work and women's work, but simply work.

When analyzed in the context of factors I have found linked to family violence, such as husband dominance in domestic decision making, sexual economic inequality, single-parent caretakers, mens' houses, and violent conflict resolution, the absence of a household division of labor by sex can tell us much about how to prevent family violence. First, it tells us that with two regular caretakers in the home, there will be regular relief from the pressures that often accompany caretaking and less chance that those pressures will boil over into violence directed at the children. Second, given our earlier finding that sibling violence is often modeled on parent-child violence, it tells us that alternative caretakers in the home will indirectly control fighting between siblings. Third, the absence of a clear division of labor by sex tells us that adult male and female roles are not rigidly defined. Thus manifestations of an unresolved male sex identity conflict both outside and within the family are unlikely. And, last, it tells us that since sexual equality accompanies the shared division of labor, each party will have the emotional and economic independence to withdraw from a potentially violent relationship.

The Central Thai, with their nonviolent ways, are living proof of the central conclusion of this study—family violence will be more common in societies in which men control women's lives, it is acceptable to resolve conflicts violently, and the mother bears the major responsibility for child rearing. The Central Thai are also living proof that it doesn't have to be this way.

Appendix A:
Methodology

This Appendix provides the details of the methodology used in the worldwide comparative research on which this book is based. Four methodological issues are covered: sampling, data collection, regional variation, and data quality.

SAMPLING

The sample used here is a revised subsample of the Human Relations Area Files Probability Sample Files (PSF; Lagace, 1979). The PSF sample contains 120 cultural groups from 60 distinct cultural/geographic regions of the world. To be included in the sampling universe for the PSF sample, a cultural group must meet two basic criteria. First, it must be a named group and a common speech community. Second, there must be at least 1,000 pages of descriptive literature providing information for at least 40 of the major topics listed in the *Outline of Cultural Materials* (Murdock et al., 1982). Specifically excluded from the universe are modern nation-states or administrative subdivisions thereof, units that constitute historical periods, units that are political empires, and units lacking detailed descriptive information for a specific community.

The sample is stratified in the sense that all groups in the universe are classified into one of the 60 cultural regions, and then two groups are randomly selected from each region. The only qualification is that all groups included in the final sample must have mutually unintelligible languages. To sum up, the PSF sample is a stratified sample of known, well-described small-scale and peasant societies of the world. Like any sample used in worldwide comparative research, it is not a true probability sample of all societies or even of all small-scale societies, since it is impossible to compile a list of all societies that should be included in the sampling universe.

As noted here, the sample used is a revised subsample of the PSF. It is a subsample in that we use 90 rather than all 120 societies. The decision to use only 90 societies was a practical one, as the HRAF data archive does not yet contain full information for all 120 societies. By revised, we mean that a few societies included in the PSF were discarded and other societies substituted in their places. Societies that were discarded, such as the Bush Negroes, Shluh, and Khasi, were discarded primarily because our pilot study indicated that there was little or no information available on the topics of interest noted here. Substitutes were selected with two criteria in mind. First, because they represent the same cultural region as a society dropped from the sample. Or, second, because they are an administrative or cultural unit in a modern nation-state, such as

Okinawa, Okayama, the Montagnais, and rural Greece. The goal in deviating from the stratified probability approach here was to increase the number of modern societies in the sample, and, thereby broaden the generalizability of the findings.

The 90 societies classified by world region are listed below.

NORTH AMERICA

Arapaho	Blackfoot	Copper Eskimo
Fox	Hare	Hopi
Iroquois	Klamath	Mam
Mescalero	Ojibwa	Papago
Pawnee	Montagnais	Tarahumara
Tlingit	Tzeltal	

SOUTH AMERICA

Araucanians	Aymara	Bororo
Cagaba	Cuna	Goajiro
Highland Quechua	Jamaicans	Mataco
Ona	Pemon	Siriono
Toba	Tucano	Yahgan
Yanoama		

OCEANIA

Aranda	Ifugao	Javanese
Kapauku	Lau	Manus
Orokaiva	Tikopia	Tonga
Toradja	Trobriands	Truk
Woleai		

AFRICA

Ashanti	Azande	Bushmen
Dogon	Ganda	Igbo
Luo	Masai	Mossi
Nuer	Pygmies	Rundi
Tiv	Zulu	

ASIA

Andamans	Bhil	Burusho
Garo	Gond	Korea
Malays	Okayama	Okinawa
Santal	Taiwan Hokkein	Tamil
Thai (Central)		

MIDDLE EAST

Amhara	Hausa	Kanuri
Kurd	Libyan Bedouin	Rwala

Somali   Teda   Tuareg
Wolof

EUROPE AND SOVIET UNION
Chukchee   Greece   Lapps
Rural Irish   Samoyed   Sarakatsani
Serbs

DATA COLLECTION

Data collection involved four steps: first, reading the ethnographic materials in the HRAF archive to locate and extract data on the variables of interest; second, coding the data into the quantitative categories set forth in Appendix B; third, conducting an intercoder reliability test to measure the consistency with which the codes were being applied; and fourth, checking and revising codes and data that fared poorly in the reliability test. The data were collected and coded by four trained coders, all members of the HRAF staff experienced in using and classifying ethnographic materials in general and materials in the HRAF data archive in particular. No attempt was made to keep the coders naive as to the ideas being tested, but the possibility of systematic coding errors in favor of or against a particular hypothesis was controlled by having one team code the family violence variables and the other team code the other variables. The coding process was guided by a project codebook, the contents of which are summarized in Appendix B, and all codes were entered on a standardized coding form.

The primary source of data was ethnographic reports in the Human Relations Area Files data archive. For a few societies, this information was supplemented by data collected from reports not in these files and from information gathered through interviews with ethnographers who had studied the society. In order to maintain some degree of unit and time focus for each sample society, coders attempted to collect as much of the data as possible from only one or two sources for each society. Of course, this was not always possible, and we make no claim that the sample is focused on a particular community at a particular point in time for each society. Along the same lines, when we found that much data was available on a society for two different points in time, a decision was made to code for only one point.

Coders were instructed to extract as much information as possible from the HRAF archive for the variable being coded. They were also instructed to consult more than one *Outline of Cultural Materials* category when searching for relevant information. Thus, for example, while the bulk of information on wife beating and husband beating is contained in category 593 (Family Relationships) additional information was found indexed under categories 578 (Ingroup Antagonisms), 586 (Termination of Marriage), 683 (Offenses Against the Person), 684 (Sex and Marital Offenses), and 837 (Extramarital Sex Relations). Some variables were coded by combining data from two or more related categories. For example, drunken wife beating was coded as absent if (1) there was a statement saying it did not occur or (2) no information about drunken wife beating and there was a statement that alcoholic beverages are not consumed in the society. For most variables, the absence of information was coded as no information. The one key exception to this rule was the coding of the husband-beating variable. If wife beating was discussed, but husband beating was not, husband beating was coded as absent. The assumption here is that if husband beating was present it would very likely have been reported, so if it is not reported it is probably absent.

Intercoder reliability was tested by having a second coder recode a randomly selected 20% subsample of the sample. Percentages of agreement were then calculated for the two sets of codes, as follows:

VARIABLE	*PERCENT AGREEMENT*
wife beating frequency	79
physical punishment of children	80
sibling aggression	95
husband beating frequency	88
severity of wife beating	83
drunken wife beating	89
intervention in wife beating	84
female work groups	73
female wealth	94
property inheritance	83
control of fruits of labor	73
marriage type	94
divorce frequency	61
household type	84
postmarital residence	89
domestic animal cruelty	66
punishment of crimes	94
pain in female initiation ceremonies	89
initiation ceremony activities	87
female fighting	94
male fighting	92
male drunken brawling	94
infanticide	100
widow remarriage freedom	78
importance of female initiation	67
female initiation ceremonies	89
menstrual taboos	67
dwelling control	86
divorce freedom	67
premarital sex double standard	94
domestic authority	78

infanticide sex preference	94
torturing the enemy	83
care of boys	83
socialization of boys	50
principal disciplinarian	61
population	100
treatment of the aged	95
men's houses	92
husband/wife sleeping arrangements	85
community exogamy/endogamy	60
warfare ethos	88
warfare goal	95

A reliability score of below 85% was considered a sign of coding problems and the two sets of codes were compared to try to identify the cause of the discrepancies. If the lack of agreement was the result of random coding errors made by the reliability coder, the original codes were allowed to stand. But if the discrepancy seemed to be the result of random errors by the first coder or the result of unclear or misapplied coding rules, all the codes were checked and recoded as necessary. Thus the final level of intercoder reliability for a number of variables is very likely higher than the foregoing percentages indicate.

As an additional check on reliability, our wife-beating codes were compared to those reported by Whyte (1978) and Justinger (1978) for societies in our sample that were also used in one of these other studies. Although Whyte measured whether wife beating was condoned or not, there is 87% agreement between the wife-beating codes for the 16 societies that appear in both samples. For the Justinger study the percentage of agreement is 83% for the 29 societies that overlap the two studies.

REGIONAL VARIATION

Ideally, relationships found between variables in worldwide comparative studies should hold for each region of the world as well as the entire sample. Testing correlations for each region allows us to identify particularly strong or weak relationships in one or two regions that might spuriously raise or lower the relationship for the entire worldwide sample. Unfortunately, such testing is not especially useful with a sample of only 90 societies with a range of from 7 to 17 societies for the seven regions represented. For this reason, formal regional variation tests are not reported. However, regional variation is considered in two other ways. First, when it is clear that a particular variable is unevenly distributed around the world, that pattern is noted where applicable in the text. Second, the mean scores for five family violence variables for the world regions are reported next. While there is general similarity from one region to another, the high frequency of child punishment in African societies, the high frequency of sibling aggression in Middle East societies, and the severity of wife beating in North American and European societies are worth noting.

	NA	SA	OC	AF	AS	ME	E
wife beating	2.5	2.3	2.4	1.9	2.3	2.5	3.0
child punishment	1.8	2.0	2.3	2.7	2.2	2.5	2.3
sibling fighting	1.5	1.3	1.9	2.0	1.6	2.7	1.5
husband beating	1.5	1.5	1.4	1.3	1.1	1.3	1.1
wife beating severity	3.6	2.0	2.9	2.9	2.1	3.0	3.5

  * NA = North America, SA = South American, OC = Oceania, AF = Africa,
 ** AS = Asia, ME = Middle East, E = Europe and Soviet Union
*** Wife beating, child punishment, and wife-beating severity are coded on a 1-4 point scale, sibling fighting and husband beating on a 1-3 point scale.

DATA QUALITY

Many people have long questioned the quality of the ethnographic data used in worldwide comparative research. There is no doubt that comparative studies are often plagued by imprecise data, missing data, and by the complexities involved in converting ethnographic materials into quantifiable codes suitable for statistical analysis. However, while people worry about these and related data problems, the problem that has drawn the most attention is systematic errors in the ethnographic information itself. Systematic errors in this context are defined as patterned inaccuracies in the ethnographic record for a number of societies, which result from characteristics of the ethnographic research process. The concern is that systematic errors influencing two variables of interest might spuriously inflate or deflate the statistical relationship between those variables.

The standard method of measuring and controlling systematic data errors is the control factor method of data quality control (Naroll, 1962). The control factor method rests on the assumption that specific characteristics of the ethnographic fieldwork process are related to the quality of the data collected. Three of these characteristics or data quality control factors are used here: sex of the ethnographer, native language familiarity, and length of stay in the field. The data quality control approach predicts that the data will be more accurate and less likely to contain systematic errors when the ethnographer speaks the native language and the more time he or she spends in the field. Following Campbell (1985) we also assume that the information on wife beating and child punishment will be more accurate if collected by a woman, since female ethnographers might have more access to women's activities than do male ethnographers. Potential data quality problems are identified by correlating the control factors with the substantive variables. If an association is found between the control factor and the substantive variables found to be related to one another, one must be concerned that the relationship is the result of systematic data errors. The effect of those errors can then be controlled through partial correlations.

The operational definitions for the three data quality control factors are as follows (Naroll et al., 1976):

SEX OF ETHNOGRAPHER

The sex of the ethnographer who collected the data on which the variable code is based.

(1) female
(2) male

LANGUAGE FAMILIARITY

Familiarity of the principal investigator with the native language of the society being studied.

(1) evidence that ethnographer did not speak the native language (use of an interpreter) or statement that ethnographer did not speak the native language
(2) evidence that the ethnographer had some knowledge of the native language (published linguistic material) or a claim that he or she spoke the native language

LENGTH OF STAY

The amount of time the principal ethnographer(s) spent collecting the data. If there is more than one principal ethnographer, the code is based on the sum of their individual stays.

(1) 1 month or less
(2) 1 to 3 months
(3) 3 to 6 months
(4) 6 to 12 months

(5) 12 to 60 months
(6) 60 months or more

The relationship (gamma) between these three control factors and the primary family violence variables are shown below.

	sex	language	stay
wife-beating frequency	−.112	−.143	−.037
child punishment	−.357	−.422	−.213
sibling aggression	−.149	−.053	.245
husband-beating frequency	.432	−.254	.299
wife-beating severity	−.016	−.548	.332
intervention	−.016	−.072	.000

These coefficients indicate that data quality is not a problem for the wife-beating frequency, sibling aggression, and intervention variables. However, the child punishment data may be influenced by the sex of the ethnographer and language familiarity, husband beating by sex of the ethnographer, and severity by language familiarity. The relationship between the quality control factors and the reporting of child punishment is not totally unexpected, as Rohner (1975) reports that another control factor—multiple verifications of informant statements—is associated with the reporting of more parental rejection and negative personality traits.

To assess further the potential impact of systematic data errors, we correlated the control factor scores with a number of substantive variables, such as female work groups, frequency of divorce, punishment of crimes, pain in female initiation ceremonies, female fighting, and men's houses, that we found associated with one or more of the three involved family violence variables. Three of the substantive variables—female work groups, female fighting, and men's houses—are positively correlated with control factors: work groups with sex, fighting with language, and men's houses with sex and language. Since, these coefficients were positive and those for child punishment negative, we can assume that systematic errors are not a source of bias in the tests of the child punishment hypotheses. And the same principle applies to the possibility of systematic errors owing to language familiarity influencing tests involving the husband-beating variable.

This leaves us with two substantive relationships that might be influenced by systematic reporting errors. First, the weak relationship (−.165) between wife-beating severity and men's houses that is weakened further (−.073) when we control for length of stay. Second, the strong relationship (.847) between husband beating and female work groups that is considerably weakened (.291) when we control for sex of ethnographer. Evidently, male ethnographers often overreport both the frequency of husband beating and the presence of exclusively female work groups.

Why this is evidently the case is not clear, although it might be that both practices are relatively unusual in Western society and therefore are more likely to be noticed and commented on by Western males.

Appendix B:
Measures and Coding Rules

Here we set forth the definitions of the theoretical variables used in the study and their operational definitions. The operational definitions are the coding rules that guided the coders in selecting the information pertaining to each variable from the ethnographies and in rating the information on the scales listed here.

Three factors guided our decisions as to what variables and measures to use and how to scale and code them. First, the hypotheses being tested, as we obviously had to select measures that seemed to be valid indicators of the theoretical concepts being studied. Our goal was to select measures with strong face validity, that is, measures that would seem to any objective observer to be reasonable indicators of the theoretical variables. Because much of the data is relatively imprecise and because some concepts are difficult to measure using secondary data, we tried to include multiple measures whenever necessary or possible. For example, we use two measures of father involvement in child rearing (men's houses and husband/wife sleeping arrangements), four measures of women's economic power, and multiple measures of each of our three sets of interpersonal violence variables.

Our second guide in selecting measures and defining them was previous worldwide comparative studies on child rearing, violence, and women's status. The most useful of these studies were Zelman (1974), Whyte (1978), and Rohner (1975). These studies provided time-saving help in determining what variables could be measured with the ethnographic data available to us, how the measures could best be scaled, and in identifying possible sources of data collection and measurement problems.

The third guide was a preliminary comparative study conducted with a sample of 45 societies (Levinson, 1981). Beyond helping clarify a variety of data collection and coding questions, the pilot study convinced us to take a behavioral rather than a normative approach in defining the variables under study. The more data we collected, the more obvious it became that not only is there more data on behaviors than on norms, values, beliefs, attitudes, and so on, but, also that the behavioral data are more trustworthy. By more trustworthy we mean that ethnographers' statements about behavior are more likely to be backed up by evidence that the behavior actually occurs, such as descriptions of wife-beating incidents, or quantitative data on the number of divorces in the community in the past year, or census counts of the number and relationships between people who live in the same dwelling. Thus the basic rule in collecting the data was to code according to what ethnographers report the people actually do, not according to what ethnographers say the people claim to do or what they should be doing.

FAMILY VIOLENCE SCALE

This measure is a gross indicator of the overall level of family violence in a society. It is computed by summing the scores for wife-beating frequency, husband-beating frequency, child punishment and sibling fighting and then dividing the total by four.

(1) 1.00 - 1.50
(2) 1.51 - 1.99
(3) 2.00 - 2.50
(4) 2.51 - 2.99
(5) 3.00 - 3.50
(6) 3.51 - 3.99

WIFE-BEATING FREQUENCY

Wife beating is the physical assault of a woman by her husband and includes hitting, slapping, kicking, throwing an object at, shoving, pushing, cutting, burning, and so on.

(1) rare or absent
(2) infrequent, occurs in 49% or less of households
(3) frequent, occurs in more than 50% of households
(4) common, occurs in all or nearly all households

PHYSICAL PUNISHMENT OF CHILDREN

Physical punishment is the use of physical violence by caretakers to punish, motivate, or discipline a child. Physical punishment is measured in terms of its frequency of use relative to the frequency of use of other socialization techniques such as scolding, instructing, rewarding, scaring, and so on. In coding this variable, you will need to examine the full range of child-rearing techniques used in each society.

(1) rare or absent
(2) infrequent, used less often in most households than all other techniques
(3) frequent, used more often in majority of households than at least one other technique
(4) common, the most frequently used technique

SIBLING AGGRESSION FREQUENCY

Sibling aggression is physical violence between nonadult siblings, regardless of age, sex, or whether or not the behavior is condoned by adults.

(1) absent or occurs in a small minority of households
(2) infrequent, occurs in a substantial minority of households
(3) frequent, occurs in a majority of households

HUSBAND-BEATING FREQUENCY

Husband beating is defined like wife beating, except that the wife is the perpetrator and the husband the target.

(1) absent or rare
(2) infrequent, occurs in a minority of households
(3) frequent, occurs in a majority of households

SEVERITY OF WIFE BEATING

Severity is based on the most severe incident reported for the society.

(1) wife beating is rare or absent
(2) painful, the severest beating is painful but causes no debilitating injury
(3) injury, the beating causes a debilitating injury such as burns or broken bones
(4) mutilation or death, the beating causes permanent injury such as loss of a limb or death

DRUNKEN WIFE-BEATING FREQUENCY

Drunken wife beating is wife beating that occurs while one or both parties is drunk.

(1) absent
(2) present with nondrunken beating also present
(3) present with nondrunken beating usually absent

TYPE OF WIFE BEATING

The reason the people in the society believe that wife beating occurs.

(1) mainly for adultery
(2) mainly for a specific reason
(3) for any reason (at husband's whim)

INTERVENTION IN WIFE BEATING

Intervention refers to steps other people take to stop or control wife beating, both in the short- and long-run. If more than one intervention occurs, use multiple codes, but circle the one that is used most often.

(1) intervention by relatives, neighbors, mediator during or immediately following a beating
(2) wife leaves temporarily and is afforded shelter by her family, neighbors, and so on immediately following a beating
(3) public censure through gossip, judicial hearing, supernatural sanction, husband pays compensation
(4) wife divorces husband
(5) intervention or divorce takes place only when abuse is serious or for unapproved reason
(6) intervention does not occur (societies in which wife beating does not occur should be coded as no information)

COMMUNITYWIDE EXCLUSIVELY FEMALE WORK GROUPS

These are groups of women who regularly work together and may include groups of female traders, women regularly working together in the fields, or routinely assisting one another in the completion of household tasks, and more organized types of work or economic arrangements.

(1) present
(2) absent

FEMALE WEALTH

Wives have independent wealth that their husbands do not control.

(1) present, women have independent income, or control wealth brought to marriage or can use portion of family income or wealth for own needs
(2) absent

PROPERTY INHERITANCE

Relative status of men versus women as heirs to economically valuable family wealth, such as land, livestock, the dwelling, or money.

(1) women preference or exclusively women
(2) roughly equal for men and women
(3) both may inherit but men have preference
(4) only men may inherit or women may inherit only in exceptional circumstances

CONTROL OVER FRUITS OF LABOR

Relative power of men and women to use products of family labor.

(1) women have exclusive or main control
(2) men and women have equal or shared control
(3) men have exclusive or main control

TYPE OF MARRIAGE

Major type of marriage actually practiced in the society.

(1) polyandry
(2) monogamy
(3) limited polygyny (under 20% of marriages)
(4) general polygyny (over 20% of marriages)

FREQUENCY OF DIVORCE

Divorce is the socially sanctioned dissolution of a marriage.

(1) rare or absent (under 5% of marriages)
(2) infrequent, or frequent in early years of
    marriage and rare thereafter (5% to 30%)
(3) moderate, a minority of couples
    (30% to 49%)
(4) common (50% to 90%)
(5) universal or nearly so (90% plus)

HOUSEHOLD TYPE

The major type of residential family unit.

(1) extended (stem, joint, lineal, fully extended)
(2) polygynous (includes compounds)
(3) nuclear
(4) mixed

POSTMARITAL RESIDENCE

The kin the newly married couple lives with or lives nearest to following the marriage.

(1) matrilocal
(2) avunculocal
(3) neolocal
(4) patrilocal
(5) mixed or no rule

DOMESTIC ANIMAL CRUELTY

Domestic animals include pets, animals raised for food products they produce (cows, goats, and so on), animals kept for labor (dogs, oxen, and so on), and animals raised for food or for raw materials (antler, fur, hair, and so on).

(1) absent
(2) treated cruelly in special circumstances (ceremonies) or limited to specific animal
(3) routinely treated cruelly

PUNISHMENT OF CRIMES AGAINST THE PERSON

Covers the socially sanctioned punishment of assault, battery, rape, and so on but does not include witchcraft, sorcery or murder.

(1) no socially sanctioned punishment
(2) punished by nonviolent means
(3) punished by both nonviolent and violent means
(4) punished by violent means

VIOLENCE OR PAIN IN FEMALE CEREMONIES

Regular use of pain in female initiation ceremonies. Societies without female ceremonies should be coded as no information.

(1) none
(2) hazing, fasting, and so on
(3) tattooing, whipping, scarification, tooth extraction, and so on
(4) genital operation

INITIATION CEREMONY ACTIVITIES

The use of pain during initiation ceremonies. The ceremony is defined broadly to include not just the ceremony but any events such as seclusion leading up to the ceremony.

(1) none
(2) nonpainful initiate activities (seclusion, training, dietary restrictions, and so on)
(3) pain infliction other than genital operation (hazing, ordeals, tattooing, scarification, tooth extraction, fasting, and so on)
(4) genital operation
(5) genital operation and other pain infliction

FEMALE FIGHTING

Physical violence between adult female residents of the community.

(1) absent
(2) present

MALE FIGHTING

Physical violence between adult male residents of the community.

(1) nonviolent, ritualized competition, or violence directed only at self or own property
(2) mix of violent and nonviolent
(3) violence directed at another person

MALE DRUNKEN BRAWLING

Physical violence between adult men in conjunction with or immediately following the consumption of alcoholic beverages.

(1) absent
(2) infrequent
(3) frequent

INFANTICIDE

The deliberate killing of an infant.

(1) absent
(2) present

WIDOW REMARRIAGE FREEDOM

Freedom of widows to remarry, on the basis of who has control over the decision to remarry and who she can remarry.

(1) widow or her relatives choose new spouse
(2) remarriage into husband's kin group preferred but not mandatory
(3) widow chooses new spouse, but from husband's kin group
(4) widow's husband's kin choose new husband
(5) remarriage strongly disapproved

RELATIVE IMPORTANCE OF FEMALE INITIATION RITES

Importance of female initiation rites relative to those of males as evidenced by degree of elaboration and community involvement.

(1) male rites are more important
(2) male and female rites both absent or equally important
(3) female rites more important

FEMALE INITIATION CEREMONIES (GUTTMAN SCALE)

This code is adapted from Young (1965) and measures the importance of initiation ceremonies.

(1) no initiations for females
(2) minimal social recognition
(3) plus personal dramatization of initiate (isolation)
(4) plus organized social response (ceremony)
(5) plus affective social response (punishment, tattooing, operations)

MENSTRUAL TABOOS (GUTTMAN SCALE)

This code is adapted from Young and Bacdayan (1967) and measures the intensity of the restrictions placed on menstruating women.

(1) no menstrual taboos
(2) rule against intercourse with menstruating women
(3) plus personal restrictions on menstruants
(4) plus stated belief that menstrual blood is dangerous
(5) plus a rule that menstruating women may not cook for men
(6) plus segregation of menstruating women from men in hut
(7) plus a rule that menstruating women may not have contact with male objects

DWELLING CONTROL (OWNERSHIP)

Ownership of the family dwelling as indicated by actual ownership, rights to dwelling in case of divorce. If dwelling is owned by the kin group, code in accord with whether it is the husband's or wife's kin.

(1) owned by wife
(2) ownership shared by husband and wife
(3) owned by husband

DIVORCE FREEDOM

The relative degree of freedom afforded men and women as indicated by rules governing divorce, who initiates divorce, number and types of reasons for divorce, and resources available to each after divorce.

(1) possible for both, but more difficult for husband
(2) equally possible or impossible for both
(3) possible for both, but more difficult for wife
(4) possible only for husband

PREMARITAL SEX DOUBLE STANDARD

Freedom to engage in premarital sex, as evidenced by specific practices (segregation, must be a virgin at marriage, and so on) which suggest a double standard favoring men.

(1) absent—equal restrictions apply or men and women have equal freedom
(2) present—more freedom for men

DOMESTIC DECISION-MAKING AUTHORITY

Authority in domestic decision making regarding day-to-day events including child care, life-style, kinship relations, and so on.

(1) wife dominates
(2) equal
(3) husband dominates

INFANTICIDE SEX PREFERENCE

(1) males more likely to be killed
(2) no preference
(3) females more likely to be killed

TORTURING THE ENEMY

The torturing of war captives by anyone in the captors' community. War captives are defined as individuals who are members of another political community.

(1) enemy not tortured, even when executed
(2) enemy tortured only in special circumstances
(3) enemy routinely tortured

PRINCIPAL DISCIPLINARIAN

The sex of the parent who has the major responsibility for disciplining a child when he or she misbehaves.

(1) usually the mother
(2) either the mother or father, but more often the mother
(3) about equally divided between mother and father
(4) either the mother or father, but more often the father
(5) usually the father

CHILD CARE RESPONSIBILITY FOR BOYS OVER 5 YEARS OF AGE

The sex of the parent who has the major responsibility for caring for male children over five years of age.

(1) usually the mother
(2) either the mother or father, but more often the mother
(3) about equally divided between mother and father
(4) either the mother or father, but more often the father
(5) usually the father

SOCIALIZATION RESPONSIBILITY FOR BOYS 5 TO 10 YEARS OF AGE

The sex of the parent who has the major responsibility for teaching male children the rules and ways of life of their society and family.

(1) usually the mother
(2) either the mother or father, but more often the mother
(3) about equally divided between mother and father
(4) either the mother or father, but more often the father
(5) usually the father

POPULATION

The population of the entire society.

(1) 0-99
(2) 100-999
(3) 1000-4999
(4) 5000-49,999
(5) 50,000-99,999
(6) 100,000-499,999
(7) 500,000-999,999
(8) 1 million-2 million
(9) 2 million plus

TREATMENT OF THE AGED

Degree of physical, material, and emotional support provided the aged.

(1) supportive treatment provided
(2) nonsupportive treatment, or combination of supportive and non-supportive treatment

MEN'S HOUSES

Buildings or places from which women are excluded and where married and single men regularly congregate, eat, and often sleep.

(1) absent
(2) present

HUSBAND AND WIFE SLEEPING ARRANGEMENTS

(1) husband and wife sleep together in the same bed
(2) husband and wife sleep together in the same dwelling but in different beds
(3) husband usually sleeps in the same bed / dwelling as wife but with regular, temporary separations for ceremonial, taboo or other reasons
(4) husband and wife sleep in separate dwellings

COMMUNITY EXOGAMY AND ENDOGAMY

Spouses regularly come from the same community or different communities.

(1) community endogamy
(2) no trend toward endogamy or exogamy
(3) community exogamy

WARFARE ETHOS

The importance of warfare to the individual as a means of gaining prestige, property or revenge. Warfare is defined here as combat between members of culturally different political communities (Otterbein, 1973).

(1) warfare is absent or rare
(2) present, but not a primary way to gain prestige, property, or exact revenge
(3) present and a primary means to gain prestige, property, or exact revenge

WARFARE GOAL (GUTTMAN SCALE)

The primary reason or reasons the society engages in warfare.

(1) warfare is absent or rare
(2) primarily defensive to protect property, and so on
(3) plus raids on individuals or small groups to exact revenge
(4) plus offensive to acquire territory or property (e.g., slaves, horses, women) or destroy the enemy

SUBSISTENCE ECONOMY

The code is taken from the *Ethnographic Atlas* (Murdock, 1967: 46-47): "A set of five digits indicates the estimated relative dependence of the society on each of the five major types of subsistence activity." Digit one = gathering, digit two = hunting, digit three = fishing and pursuit of large aquatic animals, digit four = animal husbandry, and digit five = agriculture.

In coding this variable and the following one, codes for societies in our sample provided in the *EA* should be used if the unit focus is consistent. When it is inconsistent or there is no data, the variable should be coded from the ethnographic data.

(0) 0-5% dependence
(1) 6-15%
(2) 16-25%
(3) 26-35%
(4) 36-45%
(5) 46-55%
(6) 56-65%
(7) 66-75%
(8) 76-85%
(9) 86-100%

TYPE AND INTENSITY OF AGRICULTURE

This code is taken from the *Ethnographic Atlas* (Murdock, 1967: 51) and measures the type and intensity of cultivation.

(1) agriculture is absent
(2) casual agriculture, slight or sporadic cultivation
(3) extensive or shifting cultivation, regular clearing of new fields, cultivated for a few years then allowed to fallow
(4) horticulture, semi-intensive agriculture related to vegetable gardens and fruit crops
(5) intensive agriculture, permanent fields, fertilization, crop rotation
(6) intensive irrigated agriculture

References

Adler, E. S. (1981) "The underside of married life: power, influence and violence," pp. 300-320 in L. H. Bowker (ed.) Women and Crime in America. New York: Macmillan.

Adriani, N. and A. C. Kruzt (1951) The Bare'e-Speaking Toradja of Central Celebes (The East Toradja) [Human Relations Area Files, trans.]. Amsterdam: Noord-Hollandsche Uitgeuers Maatschappij.

Alexander, R. D. (1974) "The evolution of social behavior." Annual Review of Ecology and Systematics 5: 325-383.

Allen, C. M. and M. A. Straus (1980) "Resources, power, and husband-wife violence," pp. 188-208 in M. A. Straus and G. T. Hotaling (eds.) The Social Causes of Husband-Wife Violence. Minneapolis: University of Minnesota Press.

Albert, E. M. (1963) "Women of Burundi: a study of social values," pp. 179-215 in D. Paulme (ed.) Women of Tropical Africa. London: Routledge & Kegan Paul.

Anyasodo, U. P. (1975) Ebolachi—Have You Survived the Night. Detroit: Author.

Archer, D. and R. Gartner (1984) Violence and Crime in Cross-National Perspective. New Haven, CT: Yale University Press.

Arias, I. (1984) "A social learning theory explication of the intergenerational transmission of physical aggression in intimate heterosexual relationships." Ph.D dissertation, State University of New York at Stony Brook.

Ayres, B. (1974) "Bride theft and raiding for wives in cross-cultural perspective." Anthropological Quarterly 47: 238-252.

Back, S. M., R. D. Post, and G. Darcy (1982) "A study of battered women in a psychiatric setting." Women and Therapy 1: 13-26.

Bacon, M. K., I. L. Child, and H. Barry, III (1963) "A cross-cultural study of the correlates of crime." Journal of Abnormal and Social Psychology 66: 291-300.

Baldus, H. (1937) "The social position of women among the eastern Bororo," pp. 112-162, 323-330 in Ensaios de Ethnologia Brasileira. Sao Paulo: Companhia Editora Nacional.

Baron, L. and M. A. Straus (1983) "Legitimate violence and rape: a test of the cultural spillover theory." Family Research Laboratory, University of New Hampshire. (unpublished)

Barry H., III, I. L. Child, and M. K. Bacon (1967) "Relation of child training to subsistence economy," pp. 146-158 in C. S. Ford (ed.) Cross-Cultural Approaches. New Haven: HRAF.

Barry, H., III and L. M. Paxon (1971) "Infancy and early childhood: cross-cultural codes 2." Ethnology 10: 466-509.

Barry, H., III, L. Josephson, E. Lauer, and C. Marshall (1980) "Agents and techniques for child training: cross-cultural codes 6," pp. 237-276 in H. Barry, III and A. Schlegel (eds.) Cross-Cultural Samples and Codes. Pittsburgh: University of Pittsburgh Press.

Becher, H. (1960) The Surara and Pakida; Two Yanoama Tribes in Northwest Brazil (Human Relations Area Files, trans.). Hamburg: Museum für Volkerkunde.

Belsky, J. (1980) "Child maltreatment: an ecological integration." American Psychologist 35: 320-335.

Berreman, G. D. (1978) "Scale and social relations." Current Anthropology 19: 225-237.

Bersani, C. A. and H. Chen (1988) "Sociological perspectives on family violence," pp. 57-86 in V. B. Van Hasselt et al. (eds.) Handbook of Family Violence. New York: Plenum.

Blood, R. O. and D. M. Wolfe (1960) Husbands and Wives: The Dynamics of Married Living. Glencoe, IL: Free Press.

Bowker, L. H. (1983) Beating Wife-Beating. Lexington, MA: Lexington Books.

Broude, G. J. and S. J. Greene (1983) "Cross-cultural codes on husband-wife relationships." Ethnology 22: 263-280.

Campbell, J. C. (1985) "Beating of wives: a cross-cultural perspective." Victimology: An International Journal 10: 174-185.

Campbell, J. K. (1964) Honour, Family and Patronage: A Study of Institutions and Moral Values in a Greek Mountain Community. Oxford: Clarendon.

Carlebach, J. (1962) Juvenile Prostitutes in Nairobi. Kampala: East African Institute of Social Research.

Carroll, J. C. (1980) "A cultural-consistency theory of family violence in Mexican-American and Jewish ethnic groups," pp. 68-85 in M. A. Straus and G. T. Hotaling (eds.) The Social Causes of Husband-Wife Violence. Minneapolis: University of Minnesota Press.

Carter, D. B., J. B. Dusek, M. B. Danko, and G. D. Levy (1984) "Childrearing antecedents of sex role orientation in young adults." (unpublished)

Cohen, Y. A. (1966) A Study of Interpersonal Relations in a Jamaican Community. Ann Arbor: University Microfilms.

Coleman, D. H. and M. A. Straus (1986) "Marital power, conflict, and violence in a nationally representative sample of American couples." Violence and Victims 1: 141-157.

Counts, D. A. (in press) "Female suicide and wife abuse: a cross-cultural perspective." Suicide and Life-Threatening Behavior 17.

Daly, M. (1978) Gyn/Ecology: The Metaethics of Radical Feminism. Boston: Beacon Press.

Daly, M. and M. I. Wilson (1981) "Abuse and neglect of children in evolutionary perspective," pp. 405-416 in R. Alexander and D. Tinkle (eds.) Natural Selection and Social Behavior: Recent Research and New Theory. New York: Chiron.

deSilva, W. (1981) "Some cultural and economic factors leading to neglect, abuse and violence in respect to children within the family in Sri Lanka." Child Abuse and Neglect 5: 391-405.

Divale, W. T. and M. Harris (1976) "Population, warfare and the male supremicist complex." American Anthropologist 78: 531-538.

Dobash, R. E. and R. P. Dobash (1979) Violence Against Wives. New York: Free Press.

Eekelaar, J. M. and S. N. Katz (1977) Family Violence: An Interdisciplinary Study. Toronto: Butterworths.

Ember, M. (1974) "Warfare, sex ratio and polygyny." Ethnology 13: 197-206.

Epstein, T., T. Cameron, and R. Room (1978) "Alcohol and family abuse." in Alcohol, Casualties and Crime. Report prepared for the National Institute on Alcohol Abuse and Alcoholism.

Erchak, G. M. (1984) "Cultural anthropology and spouse abuse." Current Anthropology 25: 331-332.

Erlich, V. St. (1966) Family in Transition: A Study of 300 Yugoslav Villages. Princeton: Princeton University Press.

Evans-Pritchard, E. E. (1937) Witchcraft, Oracles and Magic Among the Azande. Oxford: Clarendon.

Firth, R. W. (1936) We, the Tikopia: A Sociological Study of Kinship in Primitive Polynesia. London: Allen & Unwin.

Frayser, S. (1985) Varieties of Sexual Experience. New Haven, CT: HRAF.

Freedman, D. A. (1975) "The battering parent and his child: a study in early object relations." International Review of Psychoanalysis 2: 189-198.

Fried, J. (1952) "Ideal norms and social control in Tarahumara society." Ph.D. dissertation, Yale University.

Garbarino, J. (1977) "The human ecology of child maltreatment: a conceptual model for research." Journal of Marriage and the Family 39: 721-735.

Geertz, H. (1961) The Javanese Family. New York: Free Press.

Gelles, R. J. (1974) The Violent Home: A Study of Physical Aggression between Husbands and Wives. Beverly Hills, CA: Sage.

Gelles, R. J. (1983) "An exchange/social theory," pp. 151-165 in D. Finkelhor, R. J. Gelles, G. T. Hotaling, and M. A. Straus (eds.) The Dark Side of Families: Current Family Violence Research. Beverly Hills, CA: Sage.

Gelles, R. J. (1985) "Family violence." Annual Review of Sociology 11: 347-367.

Gelles, R. J. and C. P. Cornell (1983) International Perspectives on Family Violence. Lexington, MA: Lexington Books.

Gelles, R. J. and M. A. Straus (1979) "Determinants of violence in the family: toward a theoretical integration," pp. 549-581 in W. R. Burr, R. Hill, F. I. Nye, and I. L. Reiss (eds.) Contemporary Theories about the Family, Vol. I. New York: Free Press.

Glascock, A. P. and R. A. Wagner (1986) HRAF Research Series in Quantitative Cross-Cultural Data. Vol. II: Life Cycle Data. New Haven, CT: HRAF.

Goldstein, D. (1983) "Spouse abuse," pp. 37-65 in A. P. Goldstein (ed.) Prevention and Control of Aggression. New York: Plenum Press.

Goode, W. (1971) "Force and violence in the family." Journal of Marriage and the Family 33: 624-636.

Granzberg, G. (1973) "Twin infanticide: a cross-cultural test of a materialistic explanation." Ethos 4: 405-412.

Gray, J. P. (1985) Primate Sociobiology. New Haven, CT: HRAF.

Gregerson, E. (1982) Sexual Practices: The Story of Human Sexuality. New York: Franklin Watts.

Gusinde, M. (1931) The Fireland Indians. Vol. I The Selk'nam, On the Life and Thought of a Hunting People of the Great Island of Tierra del Fuego (Human Relations Area Files, trans.). Modling bei Wien: Verlag der Internationalen Zeitschrift "Anthropos."

Gutierrez de Pineda, V. (1950) Social Organization in LaGuajira (Human Relations Area Files, trans.). Bogotá.

Hammond, P. B. (1964) "Mossi joking." Ethnology 3: 259-267.

Hanmer, J. and S. Saunders (1984) Well-Founded Fear; A Community Study of Violence to Women. London: Hutchinson.

Henderson, R. N. and H. H. Henderson (1966) An Outline of Traditional Onitsha Ibo Socialization. Ibadan: University of Ibadan Institute of Education.

Herrenkohl, E. C., R. C. Herrenkohl, and L. J. Toedter (1983) "Perspectives on the intergenerational transmission of abuse," pp. 305-316 in D. Finkelhor, R. J. Gelles, G. T. Hotaling, and M. A. Straus (eds.) The Dark Side of Families. Beverly Hills, CA: Sage.

Hickson, L. (1986) "The social contexts of apology in dispute settlement: a cross-cultural study." Ethnology 25: 283-294.

Hilger, M. I. (1952) Arapaho Child Life and Its Cultural Background. Washington, DC: Government Printing Office.

Holmberg, A. R. (1950) Nomads of the Long Bow: The Siriono of Eastern Bolivia. Washington, DC: Government Printing Office.

Hosken, F. P. (1976) "Genital mutilation of women in Africa." Munger Africana Library Notes 36.

Hosken, F. P. (1982) The Hosken Report; Genital and Sexual Mutilation of Females. Lexington, MA: Women's International Network News.

Hotaling, G. T. and D. B. Sugarman (1986) "An analysis of risk markers in husband to wife violence: the current state of knowledge." Violence and Victims 1: 101-124.

Howe, J. (1966) Caymanian Drinking Behavior. Honors thesis, Harvard University.

Jayaratne, S. (1977) "Child abusers as parents and children: a review." Social Work 22: 5-9.

Justinger, J. M. (1978) Reaction to Change: A Holocultural Test of Some Theories of Religious Movements. Ann Arbor: University Microfilms International.

Kalmuss, D. S. (1984) "The intergenerational transmission of marital aggression." Journal of Marriage and the Family 46: 11-19.

Kalmuss, D. S. and M. A. Straus (1982) "Wife's marital dependence and wife abuse." Journal of Marriage and the Family 44: 277-286.

Keller, H. R. and D. Eerne (1983) "Child abuse: toward a comprehensive model," pp. 1-36 in A. P. Goldstein (ed.) Prevention and Control of Aggression. New York: Pergamon.

Kiev, A. (1960) "Primitive therapy: a cross-cultural study of the relationship between child training and therapeutic practices related to illness," Psychoanalytic Study of Society 1: 185-217.

Koch, K. F., J. A. Sodergren, and S. Campbell (1976) "Political and psychological correlates of conflict management: a cross-cultural study." Law and Society Review 10: 443-466.

Korbin, J. E. (1981) Child Abuse and Neglect: Cross-Cultural Perspectives. Berkeley: University of California.

Kumagai, F. (1981) "Filial violence in Japan." Victimology: An International Journal 8: 173-194.

Lagace, R. O. (1979) "The HRAF probability sample." Behavior Science Research 14: 211-229.

Lambert, W. W., L. M. Triandis, and M. Wolf (1959) "Some correlates of beliefs in the malevolence and benevolence of supernatural beings: a cross-societal study." Journal of Abnormal and Social Psychology 58: 162-169.

Landes, R. (1937) Ojibwa Sociology. New York: Columbia University Press.

Langer, W. T. (1974) "Infanticide: a historical survey." History of Childhood Quarterly: Journal of Psychohistory 1: 353-365.

Lennington, S. (1981) "Child abuse: the limits of sociobiology." Ethology and Socio-biology 2: 17-29.

Lenski, G. and J. Lenski (1970) Human Societies: An Introduction to Macrosociology. New York: McGraw-Hill.

Lester, D. (1980) "A cross-culture study of wife abuse." Aggressive Behavior 6: 361-364.

Levine, E. M. (1986) "Societal causes of family violence: a theoretical comment." Journal of Family Violence 1: 3-12.

LeVine, S. (1979) Mothers and Wives: Gusii Women of East Africa. Chicago: University of Chicago Press.

LeVine, S. and R. LeVine (1981) "Child abuse and neglect in sub-Saharan Africa," pp. 35-55 in J. E. Korbin (ed.) Child Abuse and Neglect: Cross-Cultural Perspectives. Berkeley: University of California.

Levinson, D. (1979) "Population density in cross-cultural perspective." American Ethnologist 6: 742-751.

Levinson, D. (1981) "Physical punishment of children and wifebeating in cross-cultural perspective." Child Abuse and Neglect 5: 193-195.

Levinson, D. and M. Malone (1980) Toward Explaining Human Culture. New Haven, CT: HRAF.

Lewis, I. M. (1962) Marriage and the Family in Northern Somaliland. Kampala: East African Institute of Social Research.

Loening, W. (1981) "Child abuse among the Zulus: a people in transition." Child Abuse and Neglect 5: 3-7.

Lightcap, J. L., J. A. Kurland, and R. L. Burgess (1982) "Child abuse: a test of some predictions from evolutionary theory." Ethology and Sociobiology 3: 61-67.

Lorimer, E. O. (1939) Language and Hunting in the Karakoram. London: Allen & Unwin.

Lyons, H. (1981) "Anthropologists, moralities, and relativities: the problem of genital mutilations." Canadian Review of Sociology and Anthropology 18: 499-518.

Mair, L. P. (1940) Native Marriage in Buganda. London: Oxford University Press.

Maretzki, T. W. and H. Maretzki (1963) "An Okinawan village," pp. 363-539 in B. B. Whiting (ed.) Six Cultures: Studies of Child Rearing. New York: John Wiley.

Marshall, L. (1965) "The Kung Bushmen of the Kalahari desert," pp. 241-278 in J. L. Gibbs (ed.) Peoples of Africa. New York: Holt, Rinehart & Winston.

Martin, D. (1983) Battered Wives. New York: Pocket Books.

Martin, M. J. and J. Walters (1982) "Familial correlates of selected types of child abuse and neglect." Journal of Marriage and the Family 44: 267-276.

Masamura, W. T. (1979) "Wife abuse and other forms of aggression." Victimology: An International Journal 4: 46-59.

Maxwell, R. J. and P. Silverman (1970) "Information and esteem: cultural considerations in the treatment of the aged." Aging and Human Development 1: 361-392.

McLean, S. and S. E. Graham (1982) Female Circumcision, Excision and Infibulation: The Facts and Proposals for Change. London: Minority Rights Group.

Metzger, D. (1964) "Interpretation of drinking performances in Aguacatenango." Chicago: University of Chicago, Library Department of Photoduplication, Microfilm Thesis No. T10465.

Minturn, L. and W. Lambert (1964) "The antecedents of child training: a cross-cultural test of some hypotheses," pp. 343-346 in L. Minturn and W. Lambert (eds.) Mothers of Six Cultures. New York: John Wiley.

Minturn, L. and J. Stashak (1982) "Infanticide as a terminal abortion procedure." Behavior Science Research 17: 70-90.

Minturn, L., M. Grosse, and S. Haider (1969) "Cultural patterning of sexual beliefs and behaviors." Ethnology 8: 301-318.

Morgan, P. (1982) "Alcohol and family violence: a review of the literature," pp. 223-259 in Alcohol Consumption and Related Problems, Alcohol and Health Monograph No. 1. Washington DC: Government Printing Office.

Munroe, R. H. and R. L. Munroe (1980) "Household structure and socialization practices." Journal of Social Psychology 111: 293-294.

Munroe, R. L., R. H. Munroe, and J.W.M. Whiting (1981) "Male sex-role resolutions," pp. 611-632 in R. H. Munroe, R. L. Munroe, and B. B. Whiting (eds.) Handbook of Cross-Cultural Human Development. New York: Garland.

Muratoria, B. (1981) "Protestantism, ethnicity, and class in Chimboraza," pp. 506-534 in N. E. Whitten (ed.) Cultural Transformations and Ethnicity in Modern Ecuador. Urbana: University of Illinois.

Murdock, G. P. (1949) Social Structure. New York: Macmillan.

Murdock, G. P. (1967) Ethnographic Atlas. Pittsburgh: University of Pittsburgh Press.

Murdock, G. P. et al. (1982) Outline of Cultural Materials. New Haven, CT: HRAF.

Naroll, R. (1962) Data Quality Control. New York: Free Press.

Naroll, R. (1969) "Cultural determinants and the concept of the sick society," pp. 128-155 in S. C. Plog and R. B. Edgerton (eds.) Changing Perspectives in Mental Illness. New York: Holt, Rinehart & Winston.

Naroll, R. (1970) "What have we learned from cross-cultural surveys." American Anthropologist 72: 1227-1288.

Naroll, R. (1983) The Moral Order. Beverly Hills, CA: Sage.

Naroll, R., G. L. Michik, and F. Naroll (1976) Worldwide Theory Testing. New Haven, CT: HRAF.

Nkpa, M.K.V. (1981) "Social change and problems of parent abuse in a developing country." Victimology: An International Journal 6: 167-174.

O'Brien, J. E. (1971) "Violence in divorce prone families." Journal of Marriage and the Family 30: 692-698.

O'Leary, D. K. (1988) "Physical aggression between spouses: a social learning theory perspective," pp. 31-55 in V. B. Van Hasselt et al. (eds.) Handbook of Family Violence. New York: Plenum.

Oliver, J. E. and A. Taylor (1971) "Five generations of ill-treated children in one family pedigree." British Journal of Psychiatry 119: 473-480.

Ottenberg, S. (1968) Double descent in an African society; the Afikpo village-group. American Ethnological Society, monograph 37. Seattle: University of Washington Press.

Otterbein, C. S. and K. F. Otterbein (1973) "Believers and beaters: a case study of supernatural beliefs and child rearing in the Bahama Islands." American Anthropologist 75: 1670-1681.

Otterbein, K. F. (1973) "The anthropology of war," pp. 923-958 in J. J. Honigmann (ed.) Handbook of Social and Cultural Anthropology. Chicago: Rand McNally.

Pagelow, M. D. (1981) "Factors affecting women's decisions to leave violent relationships." Journal of Family Issues 2: 391-414.

Pagelow, M. D. (1981) Women-Battering: Victims and Their Experiences. Beverly Hills, CA: Sage.

Pagelow, M. D. (1984) Family Violence. New York: Praeger.

Pasternak, B., C. R. Ember, and M. Ember (1976) "On the conditions favoring extended family households." Journal of Anthropological Research 32: 109-123.

Paulme, D. (1940) Social Organization of the Dogon. (Human Relations Area Files, trans.). Paris: Edirtrions Demat-Montchrestien, F. Louiton et Cie.

Petersen, L. R., G. R. Lee, and G. J. Ellis (1982) "Social structure, socialization values, and disciplinary techniques: a cross-cultural analysis." Journal of Marriage and the Family 44: 131-142.

Phillips, H. P. (1966) Thai Peasant Personality: The Patterning of Interpersonal Behavior in the Village of Bang Chan. Berkeley: University of California.

Pillemer, K. A. and R. S. Wolf [eds.] (1986) Elder Abuse: Conflict in the Family. Dover, MA: Auburn House.

Pospisil, L. J. (1958) Kapauku Papuans and Their Law. New Haven, CT: Yale University Department of Anthropology.

Prescott, J. W. (1975) "Body pleasure and the origins of violence." Bulletin of the Atomic Scientists 31: 10-20.

Prothro, E. T. (1960) "Patterns of permissiveness among preliterate peoples." Journal of Abnormal and Social Psychology 61: 151-154.

Pryor, F. L. (1977) The Origins of the Economy. New York: Academic Press.

Reichel-Dolmatoff, G. (1951) The Kogi: A Tribe of the Sierra Nevada de Santa Marta, Colombia, Vol. 1. Instituto Etnologico Nacional, Revista.

Rodman, H. (1972) "Marital Power and the Theory of Resources in Cultural Context." Journal of Comparative Family Studies 3: 50-59.

Rohner, R. P. (1975) They Love Me, They Love Me Not: A Worldwide Study of the Effects of Parental Acceptance and Rejection. New Haven, CT: HRAF.

Rohner, R. P. (1986) The Warmth Dimension. Beverly Hills, CA: Sage.

Rosenbaum, A. (1986) "Of men, macho, and marital violence." Journal of Family Violence 1: 121-129.

Russell, E. W. (1972) "Factors of human aggression: a cross-cultural factor analysis of characteristics related to warfare and crime." Behavior Science Notes 8: 275-312.

Sanday, P. R. (1981) "The socio-cultural context of rape: a cross-cultural study." Journal of Social Issues 37: 5-27.

Sanders, I. T. (1962) Rainbow on the Rock: The People of Rural Greece. Cambridge: Harvard University Press.

SAS Institute (1982) SAS User's Guide, 1982 Edition. Cary, NC: Author.

Savishinsky, J. S. (1976) Stress and Mobility in an Arctic Community: The Hare Indians of Colville Lake, Northwest Territories. Ann Arbor: University Microfilms International.

Schlegel, A. (1972) Male Dominance and Female Autonomy. New Haven, CT: HRAF.

Schlegel, A. and H. Barry III (1980) "Adolescent initiation ceremonies: a cross-cultural code," pp. 277-288 in H. Barry, III and A. Schlegel (eds.) Cross-Cultural Samples and Codes. Pittsburgh: University of Pittsburgh.

Segall, M. H. (1983) "Aggression in global perspective: a research strategy," pp. 1-43 in A. P. Goldstein and M. H. Segall (eds.) Aggression in Global Perspective. New York: Pergamon.

Shapiro, J. R. (1972) Sex Roles and Social Structure Among the Yanoama Indians of Northern Brazil. Ann Arbor: University Microfilms.

Silvers, L., C. Dublin, and R. S. Lourie (1969) "Does violence breed violence? Contributions from a study of the child abuse syndrome." American Journal of Psychiatry 126: 404-407.

Simmons, L. W. (1945) The Role of the Aged in Primitive Society. New Haven, CT: Yale University Press.

Sipes, R. G. (1973) "War, sports, and aggression: an empirical test of two rival theories." American Anthropologist 57: 64-86.

Skinner, E. P. (1964) The Mossi of the Upper Volta; The Political Development of a Sudanese People. Stanford: Stanford University Press.

Skrefsrud, L. O. (1942) Traditions and Institutions of the Santals (Human Relations Area Files, trans.). Oslo: Oslo Ethnografiske Museum.

Spiegal, J. R. (1981) "Ethnopsychiatric dimensions in family violence," pp. 79-89 in M. R. Green (ed.) Violence and the Family. Boulder, CO: Westview.

Spiro, M. E. and R. G. D'Andrade (1958) "A cross-cultural study of some supernatural beliefs." American Anthropologist 60: 456-466.

Stacey, W. and A. Shupe (1983) The Family Secret. Boston: Beacon.

Stark, E. and A. H. Flitcraft (1985) Spouse Abuse. Atlanta: Centers for Disease Control, Violence Epidemiology Branch.

Stark, E. and I. J. McEvoy (1970) "Middle-class violence." Psychology Today 4: 52-54.

Stark, E., A. H. Flitcraft, D. Zuckerman, A. Gray, J. Robinson, and W. Frazier (1981) Wife Abuse in the Medical Setting: An Introduction to Health Personnel. Washington DC: National Clearinghouse on Domestic Violence.

Straus, M. A. (1977) "Societal morphogenesis and intrafamily violence in cross-cultural perspective," pp. 717-730 in L. L. Adler (ed.). Issues in Cross-Cultural Research. New York: Annals of the New York Academy of Sciences 285.

Straus, M. A. (1980) "Wife-beating: how common and why," pp. 23-36 in M. A. Straus, and G. T. Hotaling (eds.) The Social Causes of Husband-Wife Violence. Minneapolis: University of Minnesota.

Straus, M. A. (1983) "Ordinary violence, child abuse, and wife-beating: what do they have in common," pp. 213-234 in D. Finkelhor, R. J. Gelles, G. T. Hotaling, and M. A. Straus (eds.) The Dark Side of Families. Beverly Hills, CA: Sage.

Straus, M. A. (1985) "Methodology of collaborative cross-national research on child abuse." Family Research Laboratory, University of New Hampshire. (unpublished)

Straus, M. A., R. J. Gelles, and S. K. Steinmetz (1980) Behind Closed Doors: Violence in the American Family. New York: Anchor.

Sverdrup, H. V. (1938) With the People of the Tundra (Human Relations Area Files, trans.). Oslo: Gyldendal Norsk Forlag.

Swartz, M. J. (1958) "Sexuality and aggression on Romonum, Truk." American Anthropologist 60: 467-486.

Turnbull, C. (1965) Wayward Servants: The Two Worlds of the African Pygmies. Garden City, NY: Natural History.

Ulbrich, P. and J. Huber (1981) "Observing parental violence: distribution and effects." Journal of Marriage and the Family 43: 623-631.

Wagley, C. (1941) The Social and Religious Life of a Guatemalan Village. Menasha, WI: American Anthropological Association.

Warner, R. L., G. R. Lee, and J. Lee (1986) "Social organization, spousal resources, and marital power: a cross-cultural study." Journal of Marriage and the Family 48: 121-128.

Wathan, Maria V. (n.d.) "A cross-cultural analysis of family organization and the severity of pain inflicted on children." (unpublished)

Whitehurst, R. N. (1974) "Alternative family structures and violence-reduction," pp. 315-320 in S. K. Steinmetz and M. A. Straus (eds.) Violence in the Family. New York: Harper & Row.

Whiting, B. B. (1965) "Sex identity conflict and physical violence: a comparative study." American Anthropologist 67: 123-140.

Whiting, J. W. M. (1960) "Resource mediation and learning by identification," pp. 112-126 in I. Iscoe and H. Styevenson (eds.) Personality Development in Children. Austin: University of Texas.

Whiting, J. W. M. (1967) "Sorcery, sin, and the superego: a cross-cultural study of some mechanisms of social control," pp. 147-168 in C. Ford (ed.) Cross-Cultural Approaches. New Haven, CT: HRAF.

Whiting, J. W. M. (1969) "The place of aggression in social interaction," in J. F. Short and M. E. Wolfgang (eds.) Collective Violence. Chicago: Aldine-Atherton.

Whiting, J. W. M. and I. L. Child (1953) Child Training and Personality: A Cross-Cultural Study. New Haven, CT: Yale University Press.

Whiting, J. W. M. and R. G. D'Andrade (1959) "A cross-cultural study of residence from infancy through marriage." (unpublished)

Whiting, J. W. M. and B. B. Whiting (1976) "Aloofness and intimacy of husbands and wives: a cross-cultural study," pp. 91-115 in T. Schwartz (ed.) Socialization as Communication. Berkeley: University of California.

Whyte, M. K. (1978a) The Status of Women in Preindustrial Societies. Princeton: Princeton University Press.

Whyte, M. K. (1978b) "Cross-cultural codes dealing with relative status of women." Ethnology 2: 211-237.

Wilkinson, L. (1986) SYSTAT: The System for Statistics. Evanston, IL: SYSTAT.

Wolfgang, M. E. and F. Ferracuti (1967) The Subculture of Violence: Toward an Integrated Theory of Criminology. London: Tavistock.

Yllö, K. (1983) "Sexual inequality and violence against wives in American states." Journal of Comparative Family Studies 14: 67-86.

Yllö, K. (1984) "The status of women, marital equality and violence against wives." Journal of Family Issues 5: 307-320.

Young, F. W. (1965) Initiation Ceremonies: A Cross-Cultural Study of Status Drama-
    tization. Indianapolis: Bobbs-Merrill.
Young, F. W. and A. Bacdayan (1967) "Menstrual taboos and social rigidity," pp. 95-110
    in C. S. Ford (ed.) Cross-Cultural Approaches. New Haven, CT: HRAF.
Zelman, E. A. (1974) Women's Rights and Women's Rites: A Cross-Cultural Study of
    Woman Power and Reproductive Ritual. Ann Arbor: University Microfilms.

Name Index

Subject Index

About the Author

David Levinson is Vice President of the Human Relations Area Files, Inc., New Haven, Connecticut. He has a MPA in nonprofit management from New York University and a Ph.D. in cultural anthropology from the State University of New York at Buffalo. His field and comparative research and publications have focused on a number of human problems, including homelessness, alcohol abuse, and crowded living conditions. He is author of more than three dozen articles and book chapters and is the senior author of *Toward Explaining Human Culture*—selected by Choice as an outstanding academic book of 1981—and *The Tribal Living Book*. He is currently writing a book on human resource development and is general editor of the *Encyclopedia of World Cultures,* to be published by Sage in 1990.

NOTES

NOTES

NOTES

NOTES

DATE DUE / DATE DE RETOUR

OCT 27 1997			
NOV 05 1997			
NOV 17 1997			
FEB. 28 1998			
OCT. 29 1998			
NOV. 12 1998			
NOV. 26 1998			
MAR. 31 1999			
NOV. 06 2000			
NOV. 14 2000			
JAN 26 2003			